# NATURAL STYLE
## FOR GARDENS

# NATURAL STYLE
## FOR GARDENS

# FRANCESCA GREENOAK

SOMA
san francisco

*For Barbara, whose garden is an inspiration*

First published in 1998 by Mitchell Beazley,
an imprint of Reed Consumer Books Limited,
Michelin House, 81 Fulham Road,
London SW3 6RB. North American edition published 1998 by
SOMA Books, by arrangement with Mitchell Beazley.

SOMA Books is an imprint of Bay Books and Tapes, Inc.
For information address: Bay Books and Tapes, 555 De Haro St.,
No 220, San Francisco, CA 94107.

For the Mitchell Beazley edition:
**Executive Editor:** Alison Starling
**Executive Art Editor:** Vivienne Brar
**Senior Editor:** Michèle Byam
**Art Editor:** Debbie Myatt
**Production:** Rachel Staveley
**Picture Research:** Emily Hedges
**Illustrator:** Vanessa Luff
**Index:** Ann Barrett

For the SOMA edition:
**Publisher:** James Connolly
**Art Director:** Jeffrey O'Rourke
**Editorial Director:** Clancy Drake
**North American Editor:** Carolyn Miller
**Horticultural Consultant:** Barbara Ellis

Library of Congress copyright-in-publication data
on file with the publisher

ISBN 1-57959-033-0

Printed in China
10 9 8 7 6 5 4 3 2 1

Distributed to the trade by Publishers Group West

# CONTENTS

## WHAT IS A NATURAL GARDEN? 6

## CREATING A NATURAL GARDEN 42

## USING A NATURAL GARDEN 94

# WHAT IS A NATURAL GARDEN?

The natural garden acknowledges the individuality of the garden terrain and the character and period of the house, working with nature to create an orderly exuberance of plants and texture. Focus is placed on associations of wild species that are easy to grow and garden cultivars that naturalize readily. Gardening in a natural style is a refinement of the skills of using plants that are well suited to the local conditions, so that with a light and lyrical hand you can orchestrate a succession of flowers and foliage that flows with both the weather and the seasons.

*Left* A drift of blanket flowers (*Gaillardia* x *grandiflora*), coneflowers, and red-flowered Salvia microphylla makes a dazzling high-summer eruption of color. Both have long, late-flowering seasons and tolerate poor soil.

N o garden is dull: Even the smallest ones have several
different habitats and microclimates within them. There
will be a shady place, a dry, sunny, hot spot, maybe a
pool or at least an area of dampness. There could be a hedge
or a wall, possibly some paving. Almost all of these—in fact
everything except rich, fertile, loamy beds—are usually regarded
as problem places, but in fact each has a specific flora that will
thrive there, opening a wealth of possibility to the enthusiast.

*Opposite* **Grasses
continue to look
glamorous throughout
the autumn and winter
months. Here, pampas
grass (*Cortaderia*)
teamed with yucca looks
sensational against
reddening maples.**

# Working with nature

This book explores a garden's underlying potential
and how to use it to redesign the garden to your
own taste. There are more than 60,000 plants in
current cultivation in the temperate world, more
than enough to suit every soil and situation. If you
match the plant to the place, you are more likely to
end up with a garden that is healthy and thriving.

A natural garden contains plants that are either
hardy natives or introductions that have naturalized
and spread. Taking its cue from the environment, a
natural garden uses plants that come from similar
habitats throughout the temperate world.

It is more rewarding, as well as easier, to work
with the forces of nature. Take a look at your
garden within the larger landscape. Some gardens
are in regions that already have a dominating
character, such as a dry, sandy coastline, a
deciduous woodland, or a rocky high-altitude
region. Gardens such as these are easy to plan
and plant, because you can see wild plants that
are blooming in the area, and use them to select a
wider range of species with similar requirements.
Seaside gardens, for example, require plants that
will survive salt spray, yet the maritime climate
is generally milder, allowing you to consider
growing plants that could be at risk inland.

In urban and suburban areas, it is often
difficult to know what kind of soils and conditions
exist. It is here that existing vegetation and even
weeds can help, because they signal the state and
quality of the land in which they are growing.

*Left* **These stone steps are colonized with woodland mosses,
ferns, sedges, and woodland-edge flowering plants such as
red catchfly (*Silene dioica*). Plants such as these naturalize
readily and should be planted, as here, in open groupings.**

# Natural balance

In the natural garden, climate as well as geography must be taken into account. Plants have their own specialties. Some, ideally suited to mild temperate regions, need a long season to flower and fruit, while others will thrive in the short but intensive summers of high latitudes. One range of species (the native flora of the Pacific Northwest, for example) can cope with winters that alternate between cold and wet. Other groups, such as alpines, die under such conditions, but will survive a greater degree of cold, provided they have a blanket of snow. Species with special xerophytic characteristics perform best in great heat. Gardening in a more natural way, you learn to note plants that are comfortable in their site and soil and that will grow well without the need for special care such as fertilizing and watering. Plants that are species, or close to species, rather than a specially selected cultivar, generally grow without much interference. The most important thing is to choose a suitable spot, giving the plant the proper soil and exposure and enough space to grow. It is also beneficial to minimize the competition from grass and weeds while the plants settle in, and to keep up the general fertility of the soil with organic matter such as compost. When treated this way, most plants thrive with a minimum of intervention.

In the natural garden, heavy-blooming plants such as African marigolds and petunias are not fed with regular applications of high-octane fertilizer throughout the season. Not only does much of the

*Below* **Warmth, scent, and texture in an informal grouping ranged around a sundial under the high summer sun: French lavender (***Lavandula stoechas***), spiky *Eryngium giganteum*, *Helianthus*, and the velvet, dark red, strongly perfumed gallica rose 'Tuscany Superb.'**

fertilizer get washed away into the water system, but fertilization also yields fast, succulent growth that tends to attract aphids.

## Garden health

There is now a strong body of research to demonstrate the benefit of a more natural approach to gardening, although some gardeners still find this hard to believe. In practice, once a garden is filled with a good balance of many different kinds of plants, you are unlikely to be greatly troubled by pests and diseases. A healthy mix of many different kinds of plants is always better than a monoculture, which tends to attract specialized pests in large numbers. For example, a formal rose garden is much more prone to problems than are roses, especially disease-resistant ones, mixed in with perennials, herbs, and shrubs. As doubts are raised about the safety of a number of garden chemicals, many people are switching to a minimum-dose regime or doing without chemicals altogether.

An important indicator of the health of any garden is its wildlife. I find that the presence of insects in the garden has become one of my greatest pleasures. It is fascinating to discover that a shrub border on your property is home to the brightly colored viceroy butterfly (*Basilarchia archippus*), whose larvae feed on willows, poplars, and a variety of fruit trees, or that the ivy on a wall provides a source of food and shelter for a number of birds and butterflies. In most parts of the country it is fairly easy to attract hummingbirds: You can buy a variety of perennials and vines that will appeal to them, including bee balm (*Monarda didyma*) and trumpet vine (*Campsis radicans*). Butterflies are easy to tempt as well: Wildflower seed firms have introduced special mixtures designed to attract these beautiful creatures.

It is useful to assess the animals with which you share your garden (*see pp. 116–29*). Some you will want to encourage, while others you may feel inclined to tolerate only in small numbers.

The larvae of several species of swallowtails (*Papilio*) feed on members of the carrot family such as dill, parsley, and carrots. You may elect to deal with them by growing extra clumps of these plants—and protecting the ones you want for the table—or by moving larvae to Queen Anne's lace (*Daucus carota*) plants in a nearby field, so they can feed and grow to maturity. On the other hand, shiny, metallic Japanese beetles (*Popillia japonica*) can be very problematic in gardens. It is important to control these pests, because their grubs chew roots of lawn grasses, and the adults destroy roses and many other flowers by chewing the leaves and flowers.

Aphids can be a problem, but if you have a good population of ladybugs, hoverflies, and praying mantises it is really not worth trying to get rid of these pests, except in the case of any plants that are especially at risk. I once experimented by treating one half of a large, aphid-infested rambling rose with a soft soap spray (which effectively disposed of the aphids), while leaving the other half untreated. A few weeks later, when the insect predators had been at work, there was no difference in foliage or flowering between the treated or untreated halves of the rose.

*Above* **Magpie moths (*Abraxas grossulariata*) vary in their patterning and are such handsome insects it seems a shame to persecute them. They lay their eggs on currant bushes, but the damage they cause is usually negligible.**

# Assessing your garden

Even the most conventional garden can adopt a more natural style that takes account of its fundamental characteristics. No changes need be hurried; the transition can be gradual or partial, entirely according to the owner's taste. The first thing to do is to take a long look at the garden as a whole, trying to determine its possibilities within its local environment.

Evaluate the garden in its own terms for the different habitats that are present within it—even if they are not all currently exploited (you might like to use the chart on the opposite page as a guide to some of the differences you should look out for). Next, consider what you might like to add to in the garden. If you do not have a pond or stream, should you think of making one? If you do, where would it fit most naturally? Similarly, you can assist any other of the microclimates you find in the garden to develop with plants of a character most appropriate to them. Perhaps there are wild plants

in your area that you would like to introduce? (However, remember that if you want truly local genetic strains, you should take seed sparingly and raise them yourself—never dig up wild plants.)

## Plants for places

The information and suggestions in this book, together with your own observations of wild places, should enable you to develop some ideas about how you want to proceed. If you have an area of dry shade, for example, you will need plants that grow best in that situation, blend well with each other, and fit into the rest of the garden. Examine the plants you already have to see which ones are growing well and therefore obviously suit the terrain. All the ideas you intend to take forward should be based on how you have related the elements within the garden, both to each other and to the character of the outside landscape.

It can be tricky to identify the exact conditions of any piece of ground: the degree of fertility; whether it is acidic, neutral, or alkaline in character; how well drained it is; and the degree of dryness or moistness. You may find help in an unexpected quarter—weeds can be very useful in indicating growing conditions. Plantains (*Plantago*) and sorrel (*Rumex acetosa* and *R. acetosella*), for example, signify acidic soil, while sow thistles (*Sonchus arvensis*) indicate alkaline conditions. Chickweed (*Stellaria media*) is a sign of neutral , well-drained soil, which is also evidenced by chicory (*Cichorium intybus*), lamb's-quarters (*Chenopodium album*), and redroot pigweed (*Amaranthus retroflexus*). Summer-flowering weeds such as mulleins (*Verbascum*) and oxeye daisies (*Leucanthemum vulgare*) indicate low fertility. Stinging nettles (*Sonchus*) and ground elder (*Aegopodium podagraria*) signify that high levels of nitrogen are present in the soil, while vetches (*Vicia*) and clovers (*Trifolium*) indicate a deficit. Areas with poorly drained soils can be identified by the presence of Joe Pye weed (*Eupatorium purpureum*), horsetails (*Equisetum*), and coltsfoot (*Tussilago farfara*).

*Below* **This garden links to the surrounding farm and woodland landscape by means of an open picket fence. Informal plantings of *Crambe cordifolia* and poplar lead the eye naturally to the countryside beyond. Crambe, with its open-branched white inflorescences, is very attractive to bees.**

## GARDEN HABITAT CHECKLIST

Check how many of these habitats you have (or could initiate) and use the relevant section of the book to help you develop them:

- **Beds:** *loamy, dry, moist; acidic/neutral/alkaline*

- **Lawn grass only:** *older lawn grasses; some wildflowers*

- **Dry shade:** *under wall/hedge/under trees*

- **Damp shade/damp wall**

- **Damp places:** *lawn or bed by faucet, pool, or boggy area*

- **Sunny places:** *bed/wall in the sun/bank*

- **Trees:** *heavy shade/light shade*

- **Longer grass:** *sun/shade*

- **Walls:** *height/material/age*

- **Fences and trellises:** *material/height/shelter*

- **Banks:** *natural/man-made; shady/bright; dry/wet*

- **Pools/ponds/streams:** *sun or shade, either still or moving*

*Left* A delightful woodland community in a city center thrives with a minimum of attention. The plants include green alkanet (*Pentaglottis sempervirens*), yellow archangel (*Lamium galeobdolon*), wood hyacinths (*Hyacinthoides*), and spotted deadnettle (*Lamium maculatum*), while ivy winds around the railings and trees.

*Below* Dry, poor soil supports a colorful mixture of plants, including purple *Veronica spicata*, blue harebells (*Campanula rotundifolia*), thyme (*Thymus*), red valerian (*Centranthus ruber*), yellow corn marigold (*Chrysanthemum segetum*), knapweed (*Centaurea nigra*), and toadflax (*Linaria vulgaris*).

# Achieving harmony in the garden

The habitats on which a natural style is based may be distant from each other in the natural landscape, but in a garden they butt up on each other and need to be linked or given points of transition in terms of planting and design. You also need to consider the style and period of the house to which the garden belongs, as well as to the wider landscape outside your immediate vicinity.

The moment you enter a garden, you should be able to detect a distinct character and how that reflects the interests and personality of the owner. The most significant plants, an unusual style of plant associations, the flow of the design, and the particular way the challenges of terrain are met reflect the preferences of the individual gardener.

Just as a piece of music can sound quite different depending on the performer, so plants will look and behave differently according to who is handling them and where they are planted. There is endless scope for originality and individuality, although it is also useful to visit other gardens, read books, and go to flower shows in order to find out what is available and how other people plant and design. Then clear your mind and plan your garden according to your own vision.

Gardeners have always loved the sensuality of the garden, and some, such as the seventeenth-century British writer William Lawson, author of the classic *The New Orchard and Garden,* have reveled in the intellectual pleasures that a garden affords. This is surely the clue to a garden that brings full satisfaction—a lifelong relationship in which your interests develop and your knowledge extends as you experiment with new plants and schemes.

One element that is almost completely absent from most writing about plants and gardens is the suggestion that the gardener as an individual might develop not only in knowledge and experience of gardening but also in terms of personal, physical, and psychological appreciation. With the increase in asthmatic complaints that depress the power to smell, fewer people are able to appreciate scents. Even nonasthmatics often hunch their shoulders, screw their necks forward, and gasp when they are about to smell something, thus preventing their sense organs from functioning properly. Fuller appreciation is likely when you simply allow the scent to flood your normal breathing, keeping the mind and the senses wholly alive to the beauty of the different strands of scent. It is the same with the other senses. If you allow your hands to become hardened and calloused and the joints stiff with overtension, you lose the acute sensibility of the fingertips. If you strain your eyes to see everything, you are more likely to give yourself a headache than to refine your perception of texture and color. If you can feel relaxed and happy in your garden, you are more likely to extend your appreciation.

*Below* **A hillside garden tumbling to a pool of yellow flag and variegated iris. The foxgloves on the edge of the trees give way to drier ground and *Lychnis coronaria*. The effect looks unplanned, but there is a careful balance of shrubs and flowers, dwarf conifers, and other evergreens.**

*Opposite* **A damp, grassy path dominated by an informal planting of *Primula florindae* and blue *Meconopsis baileyi*. To the right are the demure crimson-brown blooms of another choice woodlander, *Trillium sessile*. Dotted amongst the shrubs are kinds of woodland flora, such as wood hyacinths and Turk's-cap lilies.**

# A garden of harmonious sensuality

Scent is one of the most compelling senses, working on the subconscious by direct routes, conjuring up ideas, memories, and desires. However, when planning your garden you need to be sensitive to the power of scent. Some of the strong spring scents, such as winter honeysuckle (*Lonicera*), narcissus, and hyacinth, are made for cool, frosty air. If you bring these plants indoors their impact is so strong that it becomes almost disagreeable. On the other hand, the fleeting scent of snowdrops (*Galanthus nivalis*), the tang of daffodils, and the sweetness of grape hyacinths (*Muscari*) are better appreciated in warm indoor conditions.

There are enough scented plants not only to take you through the entire year but also to grow without the fuss and bother associated with the horticulturally demanding and more conventionally admired specimens, such as hybrid roses. If you want roses, there are many types that grow readily in seminatural conditions and are at their happiest left to themselves. These include wild species with light, sweet scents, such as the swamp rose (*Rosa palustris*) and the meadow rose (*R. blanda*), both of which will ramble cheerfully in a shrub border. One of my favorite roses is the sweetbriar (*R. eglanteria*), for the rich, musky apple scent of its leaves—although this is a species that, as with other imports from the Old World, ran riot in New Zealand. I believe that some of the delightful cultivars, developed mainly by Lord Penzance in the 1890s, may be better behaved in that region of the world, but in general sweetbriars behave well in temperate conditions. Especially delightful is the one named 'Lord Penzance' after its breeder. It has sweetly scented foliage (although the pink 'Lady Penzance' is stronger in this respect) and small, delicately sweet flowers in an unusual shade of buff-rose, blending into a rich golden center.

The rugosas are also to be treasured for their glossy apple-green foliage and scented single and double flowers. The species *R. rugosa*, originally from northern China, Japan, and Korea, has flowers that range from pale to dark pink. *R. r. alba* is also highly scented, with pure white flowers, while the outstanding hybrid 'Blanche Double de Coubert' is equally fragrant, with almost double white flowers set against dark foliage. All of these rugosas possess the useful twin qualities of thriving in poorer soils and shaded conditions and of repeat flowering.

### The tangible framework

The shapes and textures within gardens are not simply for admiring at a distance. Even if you can find very little time to sit and relax within a garden you can still enjoy them. Plant scented herbs and favorite flowers by the side of the most-used paths, so that you can reach out and rub the foliage to release their scents each time you pass by. Thymes, mints, and chamomile may be tucked between stone flagstones or paving or planted by doorsteps, so that the scent is released when

*Below* Midsummer blooming lilies of the Asiatic hybrid type characteristically hold their heads upward. Among the best are 'Apollo' and 'Sterling Star,' both white and reliable, with bowl-shaped flowers.

anyone walks over them. Some leaves and petals are irresistible—the silver soft lamb's ears of *Stachys byzantina*, the velvet leaves of alchemilla species, and the soft petals of the rose are all lovely.

Keep in mind that it is not just your hands that are sensitive. Explore the lawn in bare feet or give your toes a treat by walking through chamomile or mint. Winter sunshine is soft and warming, even through a sweatshirt or coat, and it is always pleasant to feel the elements on your face, whether it is a spring breeze or a soft drizzle.

Some trees with ornamental bark—shiny-barked species of cherry, birch, and maple—are the better for being rubbed, because this keeps them shiny and bright and free from dirt and dust. It is easy to neglect this service and let the glorious bark of these types of tree turn dowdy, so if you have a tree with ornamental or flaking bark, make sure to give it a stroke as you pass by.

## Beauty and taste

Plants grown for eating can also be of exceptional beauty. Apple trees, quince and medlars, apricots, plums, and cherries all have great decorative value, from their early leaves through to their blossoms and ripe fruits. Allowing for climatic variations, there is almost without exception a fruit tree that will grow well in your garden and need very little attention. The same applies to bushes such as gooseberries or, if you have acidic soil, high- or low-bush blueberries. Gooseberries are a greatly undervalued fruit. They come into bright green leaf very early in the season, when they are superb if underplanted with scented flame-colored or yellow tulips; the fruits may be used early, when they are still sour, or left to ripen to sweet fullness in ivory, gold, green, or red.

Many salad greens are not out of place in an ornamental garden. In my smallest gardens I have grown oak-leaved and loose-leaf lettuces in the flower borders, where they were much admired. Mache and land cress will also fit into odd spaces among flowers. Bunching onions, the easiest of onions to grow, make neat clusters, while pole beans are also pleasing to the eye.

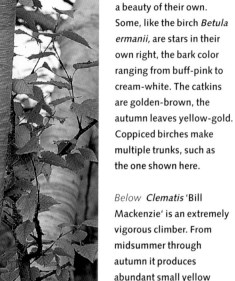

*Left* Tree trunks have a beauty of their own. Some, like the birch *Betula ermanii,* are stars in their own right, the bark color ranging from buff-pink to cream-white. The catkins are golden-brown, the autumn leaves yellow-gold. Coppiced birches make multiple trunks, such as the one shown here.

*Below* *Clematis* 'Bill Mackenzie' is an extremely vigorous climber. From midsummer through autumn it produces abundant small yellow flowers, which are followed by large seed heads, at first silken and then fluffy. It is thought to be a hybrid between two "orange peel" types of clematis, *C. orientalis* and *C. tangutica.*

Strawberry plants, especially the delicate and piquant wild and alpine strawberries, are a distinct asset in an informal garden. Growing delicious fruits, herbs, and vegetables is also a means of sharing the joys of the garden with children.

### Harmonies and sounds

While for many people the singing of birds is the archetypal sound of spring, there are resonant garden sounds throughout the year, such as the sighing of summer breezes through foliage and the thrashing of tree branches in the equinoctial gales. There is also a wide spectrum of rain sounds, from the gentle soft rains of summer showers to the lashing of storms and the brittle reports of sleet and hail, all of them creating different harmonies, depending on whether the rain is falling on leaves, water, clay or wooden tiles, or thatch.

Natural sounds can be augmented effectively by seminatural ones, set off by wind or water. While Aeolian harps are not to the taste of many gardeners, Asian deer scarers are increasing in popularity. This device consists of a poised piece of hollow bamboo that, once filled with water, seesaws to empty its load, hitting another piece of wood with a sound like a drumbeat before rebalancing and refilling. Wind chimes may be bought in different pitches in major and minor keys, while among more natural sounds, water has its own repertoire, created by a rill, a fountain, a fall, or a spout falling into a still pool.

Do not neglect the resident and visiting insects, birds, and small mammals. Listen for the buzz of different kinds of bees, the chirrups of grasshoppers and crickets, and the rattling of dragonflies and

*Left* **Lupinus** 'Noble Maiden' is a clump-forming perennial that looks superb when grown informally. Plant two or three as early-summer keynotes in a smaller area, so that they contrast with the color of plants such as these oriental poppies (*Papaver orientale*).

*Above* **The bamboo deer scarer is a means of introducing water in a garden corner that is too small for a pool or fountain. It works on a simple seesaw principle, the drips filling the hollow cavity until it pivots and drops with a sharp thud on the surrounding pebbles.**

large beetles. Sometimes you can hear the cry of a hawk or some other large bird flying over the garden, followed by the sudden disturbance it creates among the smaller birds. Tune your ear to the squeaks of tiny mammals and frogs, and catch the noises of owls and animals that come by night, identifiable only by their highly individual sounds.

## Vision and vistas

A danger with seeing a vista or part of a garden as a flat image on a book or magazine page is that one continues to perceive it in two-dimensional terms. One of the true pleasures of being inside a garden is being at leisure to walk around it, finding different vistas and focusing on different aspects, both near and far. You are no longer a remote observer turning the pages of a book but rather a participator in the garden's sensations, forming your own individual impressions.

It is also important when considering your own garden to maintain a freshness of approach. Aim for a garden that will be pleasing to all the senses and all kinds of sensibilities, letting the design grow out of the nature of the place rather than from an imposed scheme, so that the effects are more exciting and satisfying. In such a garden, the sights that meet your eye will be a regenerative and lasting source of pleasure.

*Above* **In this garden, good use has been made of interesting near and distant views. The vista, allied with billowing hedges, a linear path that leads into shadow, and the splashes of poppy red across the garden in the foreground, give the garden greater dimension.**

In the end, the garden is an individual response that takes into account your needs, ambitions, and the kind of management that you are prepared to undertake. If you are relaxed about the design and select plants that suit you in both size and form, you will need to do less pruning and general cutting back. If you match those plants to the places that suit them best, they will grow well.

However much you know about gardening, keeping the soil in good condition is always the first consideration, although tackled in a natural way this need not be too great a chore (*see pp. 142–5*).

## Modeling from nature

Even in the best gardens, many of the most beautiful effects happen by chance. The true art of the garden is to recognize and value these fortunate effects that may have been brought about by self-seeding or a particular habit of growth, or by an association of color, texture, or scent that strikes home. I grew up in a garden

*Below* **A hot-climate alpine garden dominated by dark-leaved, starlike agaves, by cape cowslips, with its succulent strappy leaves, and by ruby-red flowers, as well as a selection of low-growing sedums and sempervivums.**

where, as spring turned to summer, there was a unbelievable haze of blue, as English bluebells and naturalized American larkspur burst into bloom, filling the beds and spilling over on to the path and the driveway. I now believe that a nicely judged association of native and naturalized plants, growing harmoniously with good planning and design, is one of the most rewarding as well as one of the most easily manageable styles of gardening.

First, however, there needs to be a framework within which the garden can develop. For a garden that takes its cue from the natural world, there is no better model than the natural habitats that are being emulated. Notice plants that grow in drifts—they include many woodland genera, for example trout lilies. You will find that other plants, such as wood anemones and hepaticas, grow in smaller

*Opposite* **A simple and beautiful combination of *Erythronium revolutum* and the elegant ostrich fern *Matteuccia struthiopteris*. Both will naturalize if planted in congenial spots in moist, humus-rich soil in dappled shade.**

are fading and seeding, they will be hidden from view, but when they are in their full glory you will have a treasured area of secret garden.

A swathe of close-cropped grass next to a drift of meadow flowers and grasses also creates a sense of natural wildness being brought under orderly control. Simply mowing paths through plain grass creates a lovely contrast in color and texture.

## Theory into practice

Assessing your garden for the kinds of habitat it contains and for its prevalent climate will give you an idea of what will grow. If you put this grid together with your ideas about how the garden will be used by you and your family, while also taking into account the period and size of your house and its immediate environment, you have a rational base from which to build your design. For a truly natural style, each part of the garden should flow harmoniously into adjacent ones.

Many gardens, especially those in urban areas, are longer than they are wide, although the effect can be mitigated by making use of a design that employs lateral sweeps. Espaliered fruit trees offer a good way of making a light but definite line across a garden and may be used to mark the end of a wildflower lawn or as a backdrop to a pool. A well-placed artifact, such as a sculpture, can draw the eye, and the surrounding vegetation seems automatically to fall into a composition around it.

Some people like to draw everything out on graph paper, but this is only a good idea at a very early stage. It is far better to get out in the garden, experiencing its full dimensions and judging at first hand its widths and heights. I like either to stick bamboo stakes into the ground vertically or to lay them on the ground, with a hose mimicking the curves, to get an idea of how the intended design will actually use a space. I then look at this crude bamboo-hose arrangement, trying to imagine what the proposed design will look like from every angle through the seasons, while making adjustments according to light and shade, space, and the view from the house and garden.

*Above* **Closely mown paths wind their way through this meadow garden with its occasional trees. The spring flush of bloom is over, leaving only buttercups and flowering grasses. Mowing will leave the path neat over the fall and winter months, ready for the spring flowering.**

groups, while plants such as lilies are naturally dotted about in ones and twos, and meadow plants grow patchily interwoven in a tapestry rich with plant life.

Larger plants pay an important role. Trees and shrubs can be brought into prominence at the end of a vista, to punctuate a long border or signal a transition from one habitat to another. Hedges and arches also give height to specific areas of the garden and may be used to create a naturalistic boundary or to divide sections of the garden. If heights are varied, you can create a grassy area with a pleasantly wild feel inside a neater overall design, for example by clipping a hedge at waist height so that you can see over it. During the less attractive period before mowing, while the flowers

*Left* **Saponaria ocymoides** has small, slightly irregular flowers. It grows naturally in rocky terrain, but readily takes to growing in dry beds or on walls, where its spreading pink mats are attractive to butterflies.

*Below* **Clematis montana**, with its delightful white or pink flowers, is invaluable for north-facing walls and hedges or for growing into big trees. Vigorous and virtually trouble-free, it blooms in spring. Some cultivars are scented.

Trees and shrubs are underused in gardens. Evergreens emerge and come into their own in winter, then melt into the background during spring and summer. Trees in a lawn are always significant, while trees or climbing shrubs, making or draping across archways, create a tantalizing glimpse into another part of a garden. You can also use dainty trees (such as crab apples) to filter the gaze to another part of the garden.

Always make pathways wider than you think you will require; plants invariably sprawl over them. Remember also that however carefully and beautifully you plan and make your paths, people will always take the most direct route to your door. Therefore, do not try to be too clever—the simplest designs are usually the most effective.

## Management

The natural style of gardening should involve a minimum of labor. If hardy plants are chosen and grown in the soil and exposure in which they thrive, there should be no need for much interference. On principle, I believe in seeing how plants develop on their own, assuming their mature shapes. This tends to make for a relaxed, interesting kind of garden, although it also involves an element of risk. Occasionally I may transplant, but gardening for me is a matter of practicality as well as principle. Like most people, my gardening time is limited by

*Above* **This part of the garden is designed to capture the view to the sea; clipped conifers and neat hedges provide a perfect foil to the natural mixture of foxgloves, grasses, and the oriental poppy; stonecrop (*Sedum*), which is about to flower, is given a backdrop by the pretty foliage of pittosporum to the right.**

the demands of a busy life, leaving no time for complicated techniques or plants that require constant care. This entails a garden with a good structure that can be left if I am away or especially busy—and then brought back into good form with a minimum of work. In general, I aim for effects that can be maintained by the odd half hour here and there, and I try to make these short bursts of upkeep a pleasure. If you design a garden that is more complicated and demanding than you can easily manage, its upkeep becomes a chore and the garden itself becomes a constant reproach.

Thinking time is important, too. Consider what you are going to plant and where. Taking care with the planting itself is also well worthwhile. Container plants benefit from having at least some of the potting mix gently washed or shaken off. As roots

can be easily damaged, the plant should then be placed straight into the planting hole, which should always be larger than the extent of the roots. In this way the plants can be safely accommodated and the roots packed in and firmed with good-quality soil. I like to water my plants with a diluted solution of seaweed, because this has a beneficial effect on root growth and helps to minimize the trauma that accompanies transplanting. However, once the plant has settled in I will water only if there are exceptionally high temperatures or a prolonged spell of dry weather.

*Opposite* **The fruits of this hybrid crabapple, 'Red Sentinel,' are unpalatable to birds. A dwarf form of apple, or a species crab or mountain ash, attracts a host of birds and insects. A birdbath is a real boon for birds; ideally it should be at least 2ft (60cm) high and positioned in an open area.**

# Using natural materials

Although the twentieth century has brought us many excellent synthetic materials, natural materials tend to be more suitable for a natural-style garden. They generally look more at home outdoors and weather more satisfactorily but do require sympathetic matching with the house, the planting, and the immediate landscape.

*Right* **Rough-cut wooden planks can be used to make a simple rustic bridge to traverse a marshy area of the garden. A plank bridge is totally in keeping with an informal part of the garden and provides dry footing so that you can admire the plants as they grow.**

*Below* **A glorious stone wall gives ample foothold for a cascade of red and white valerian (*Centranthus*), while its rough surface also provides ideal niches for lavender-blue *Campanula poscharskyana* and red poppies to flourish.**

Natural materials tend to be expensive. If cost is a problem, I would always advise using less of a good-quality material rather than large quantities of something inferior. You can always add to a good base, while a compromise usually remains just that and is often costly to replace. Keep an eye open at local building supply stores for sales, as well as at house auctions and yard sales, for some exciting and possibly unusual materials at economical prices. Mixing materials is another option. A few good flagstones that do not quite cover an area can be effectively combined with less-expensive bricks, for example.

Installing materials yourself is another way to cut costs. Anyone can build a small wall or path, and building such structures yourself makes them a special pleasure because of the extra effort invested. With larger projects, it is best to hire a professional to do the skilled work, although you can participate by preparing the site. Keep in mind that the best installation method will depend on where you live. In areas where the ground freezes over winter, you'll need to lay all types of stone and brick on a 4–6in (10–15cm) deep layer of packed gravel topped by 2in (5cm) of sand. Otherwise, freezing and thawing over winter will heave stones out of place and damage mortar. In milder climates, a 2in (5cm) layer of tamped, level sand is sufficient. If you are not setting the stones in mortar, add a layer of landscape fabric on top of the sand to prevent weeds.

Out of the vast range of natural materials, some have a special association with gardens. **LIMESTONE** Soft colors and textures are the hallmark of this lovely type of stone. Use limestone for dry-laid stone walls, edgings, and paving. It is also used for sculptures and containers such as urns. Keep in mind that limestone rarely looks its best in areas where another type of stone is more prominent. **SANDSTONE** This widespread stone comes in a wide range of colors, including grays and yellows. If you look closely, you can see the tiny

compressed particles of sand in the rock. The fact that it can be crumbly or flaky does not detract from its appeàl. Use sandstone for plant-covered walls— especially fern ones— paving, and sculpture.

**GRANITE** This hard-wearing sparkling rock is nicer left rough or semipolished than mirror polished. Use rough boulders for edging informal paths. It comes in reds, pinks, blues, and green-grays. Often used in the form of small rectangular Belgian blocks in the garden, it can be cold, but grass growing between the blocks looks very attractive. Use granite for paving and stone walls. It is also used for garden artifacts such as sculpture and small fountains.

**BLUESTONE** This is a dense, fine-grained type of sandstone. As its name suggests, bluestone most often comes in blue- or gray-black. It is commonly cut into squares or rectangles and used as rough-hewn paving stones. Because of its rougher surface, it is less slippery when wet than somewhat similar-looking slate. It is also less expensive. Use it for paving, or as thick slabs for making rustic benches or tables.

**SLATE** This elegant stone comes in colors from charcoal to a beautiful blue-gray or dark pink. It is especially attractive used as flagstone in sunny areas, particularly when edged with brick for contrast. A slab of slate also can be used as an unusual table top or bench.

*Above* **A hilly woodland walk, with steps held secure by pine trunks wrapped with wire mesh to prevent their becoming slippery. The dark foliage of ferns and shrubs is lit up by lilies, garden columbines (*Aquilegia*), Welsh poppies (*Meconopsis cambrica*), rhododendrons, and common bugleweed (*Ajuga reptans*).**

*Above left* **A stone wall in summer, generously colonized with navelwort (***Umbilicus rupestris***), with its flat round leaves and small turrets of green flowers; ivy-leaved toadflax (***Cymbalaria muralis***), dotted with tiny purple and cream snapdragons; and the fern, maidenhair spleenwort (***Asplenium trichomanes***).**

*Above right* **A water sculpture in Monterey, California by Daryl Stokes, made in an old tree. Water falls from metal bowls, fixed into the crevices of the trunk, and splashes into a pool at the base. The sculptor makes similar falls with large pieces of driftwood.**

**WOOD** Versatile and attractive, wood is suitable for benches, retaining walls, fences, and decks that all are in character for a natural-style garden. Make wooden bench seats with brick, stone, or wood supports. Some wooden furniture is tough enough to be left outdoors, and it weathers nicely. (Check that exotic hardwoods such as teak come from managed forests.) Logs make effective sides for raised beds and can be used as well as retaining walls or steps. Split-rail fences are natural looking, too, and make quite effective supports for climbing roses and vines such as clematis. For a more cottage-style look, consider a picket fence painted white. Decks also are effective additions to natural-style gardens. Plan them to provide a transition between house and garden, as well as to create a restful place to enjoy the outdoors.

**BRICK** Lovely for paths, walls, and edging strips, brick is attractive when used alone or in combination with other types of stone. Winter freezing and thawing will cause softer bricks to flake, making them unsuitable for paths. Select a grade of brick suitable for the severity of the winters in your area. There are any number of patterns you can use. One to consider is repeated groupings of two or three laid one way and the same number laid at right angles. Either lay bricks in mortar or simply butt them together, which means plants will spring up in the cracks. You may find old used bricks at demolition sites or at retailers that sell used architectural supplies.

**CONCRETE** Although not strictly a natural material, concrete pavers are easy to install and weather decoratively. Use them for stepping stones or paving. Pavers that resemble log "rounds" are especially attractive. Concrete is also used for urns, garden sculpture, and other ornaments.

**CAST IRON, WROUGHT IRON** Cast-iron garden furniture and fittings were the vogue in the nineteenth century; their popularity has now come full circle, and reproductions of traditional designs are now widely available. You may find antiques at retailers that specialize in garden items. Wrought iron was typically used for making gates, railings, and balustrades, but pillars and other plant supports are available, too. Iron fixtures are very attractive when draped with vines such as morning glories, clematis, or climbing roses.

**STONES, GRAVEL, PEBBLES** These should be used sparingly to match with the house textures and colors and the immediate environment. Pebble paths are lovely in seaside gardens. Pebble beaches around water features look natural as long as they blend in with the surroundings.

## HOW TO MAKE A SOD SEAT

Herb seats date back to the Middle Ages, but are useful and inviting in modern gardens. They consist of a support in brick or stone (a rectangular, open-topped box of bench size and proportions) almost filled with rubble, then topped with a layer of soil that is planted with fragrant herbs, such as chamomile or thyme, or even with pieces of sod. Seat backs and arms can be added if desired.

1 When you have decided on a site for your seat, dig foundations 12in (30cm) deep—a little wider than the wall that will be built on top of it. Fill the trench with rubble (broken bricks, tiles, and stones) and concrete it over, so that it is smooth and level with the ground.

2 Build a brick or stone box over the foundations up to the height you want. Fill the box with rubble, then small stones and grit (to stop soil particles being washed down into the rubble), before filling the top with 9–12in (23–30cm) of weed-free topsoil.

3 Smooth and firm the surface of the soil and lay pieces of sod, or plant with herbs spaced about 2½in (7cm) apart. Use the seat once the plants have become established (see the finished seat on the right). Do not forget to water during dry spells. Trim the plants with hand pruners as necessary.

*Right* This herb seat at Sissinghurst, in England, is nicknamed "Edward the Confessor's chair." It was built by Harold Nicolson and Vita Sackville-West's chauffeur with bits of masonry from the old house at Sissinghurst. It is planted with the nonflowering chamomile 'Treneague,' with thyme in the paving stones round about, and daphne and foxglove to the side.

# Special conditions

The broad groups of habitat described so far may be found or created in most places. Some gardens, however, have special conditions that would be difficult or even impossible to replicate elsewhere. If you are after a conventional kind of garden, with beds and a standard hedge, extreme conditions may seem to be a severe impediment. If, however, you opt for a natural approach, you will be able to create a beautiful garden that has a style of its own and is easy to care for, too. The elegant grass gardens of parts of the coastal United States are good examples of this type of garden. In Britain, the celebrated gardener Beth Chatto, at the outset of her gardening career, almost despaired of a dry, scorched part of her garden, where as she recalls

*Below* **A shaded north-facing border, backed by a holly hedge, owes its appearance to the textures of the feathery fennel foliage (*Foeniculum vulgare*), the spear-shaped leaves of *Iris orientalis,* and the mounded clumps of flowering *Geranium phaeum* and *Brunnera macrophylla.***

"even native weeds perished." She decided to borrow from both Mediterranean and American gardens, as well as from natural habitats, and now her dry gardens are world famous.

## Coastal gardens

Coastal gardens are among the most beautiful anywhere, although gardening books generally present them as problem cases. This is because salt-laden winds make it especially difficult for inland plants to survive in them.

One of the most effective, simple gardens I have seen is on the windswept Suffolk coast in eastern England. This area is notorious for its harsh weather conditions, and the owners also have to contend with high tides bringing the sea and its detritus to the gate and sometimes into the garden. However, instead of getting rid of the pebbles, the owners have imported more of them from the beach and planted coastal horned poppies (*Glaucium flavum*) and sea kale (*Crambe maritima*) on the gravel, and sea lavender (*Limonium vulgare*) in a pocket of soil. There is also *Erigeron* 'Charity,' with its pink daisylike flowers, mounds of silver santolina, and sea holly (*Eryngium*). Above the low pebble wall, tamarisk trees (*Tamarix gallica*), flowering crimson and pale peach, are used to break the force of the wind, while wild roses offer a second line of defense.

Even a garden that is practically all rock can be made beautiful by the encouragement of native alpine plants and the addition of extra species that enjoy similar conditions. Small pockets of soil, given extra humus, will make a naturalistic bed. Depressions in the rock, given some soil, can be planted with salt-tolerant species such as sea thrift (*Armeria maritima*), vivid blue squills (*Scilla*), woolly yarrow (*Achillea tomentosa*), and trailing plants such as rock cress (*Arabis*), rock soapwort

*Opposite* **A glorious view across a bay is here seen through an informal grouping of borage (*Borago officinalis*), pot marigold (*Calendula officinalis*), dog daisy (*Leucanthemum vulgare*), and fennel (*Foeniculum vulgare*).**

(*Saponaria ocymoides*), and humps of sea campion (*Silene maritima*). Areas that catch the sunshine will gain extra warmth from the hot rock, permitting hot-climate species, while shady places that are partly damp will support ferns.

## Windy places

In the Great Plains and on exposed windy sites, a gardener can choose a spare, totally natural effect that takes its cue from the surrounding landscape. Boundary walls and hedges may be given additional depth by trees and shrubs, which make the best windbreaks, filtering the wind and slowing and softening it. Sycamore maple (*Acer pseudoplatanus*) will survive very strong, cold winds, and also good are green ash (*Fraxinus pennsylvanica*), white willow (*Salix alba*), and oaks such as bur oak (*Quercus macrocarpa*). In mild areas you can indulge in plants such as golden trumpet tree (*Tabebuia chrysotricha*), California laurel (*Umbellularia californica*), and cordylines (*Cordyline australis*). Once a fairly dense windbreak is in place, the garden within will be warmer and more humid and capable of playing host to a wider range of plants. The bright *Geranium sanguineum*, the silvery artemisia (*Artemisia absinthium* 'Lambrook Silver'), and purple coneflower (*Echinacea purpurea*) are among those plants that stand up well to windy conditions.

## Protection from pollution

Windbreaks are invaluable in noisy, polluted urban areas, too. Large gardens can be protected from both fumes and traffic noise by an informal border of trees and shrubs planted two or three deep. A good thick hedge will do a lot to bring peace to a smaller garden. There is a wide range of plants that tolerate a certain level of pollution, such as black locust (*Robinia pseudoacacia*), flowering quinces (*Chaenomeles*), European and North

*Left* **Heaths, growing as they should in a naturalistic way, in a sandy, heathy landscape with scattered trees. This particular species of heath is *Erica* x *darleyensis* 'Margaret Porter,' which flowers in late winter and early spring.**

American serviceberries (*Amelanchier*), mock oranges (*Philadelphus*), cotoneasters, and spiraeas. Climbing plants that also tolerate polluted air include scarlet-flowered trumpet vine (*Campsis radicans*) and charming, white-flowered climbing hydrangea (*Hydrangea anomala petiolaris*), which also is valued for its shade tolerance. Among the large number of perennials to choose from are the large-leaved bergenias, dainty bleeding hearts (*Dicentra eximia* and *D. formosa*), wood spurge (*Euphorbia amygdaloides*), and false Solomon's seal (*Smilacina racemosa*), as well as most of the coneflowers (*Rudbeckia*), comfries (*Symphytum*), and meadow rues (*Thalictrum*).

### Dry shady places

Dense overhead trees, especially those with shallow roots, create dry, shady spots. Sites underneath the eaves of a house, especially on the side away from the prevailing winds, also are commonly dry and shady. Among shrubs that tolerate dry conditions are English holly (*Ilex aquifolium*), common snowberry (*Symphoricarpos albus*), jetbead (*Rhodotypos scandens*), and five-leaf aralia (*Acanthopanax sieboldianus*), as well as flowering raspberry (*Rubus odoratus*). Vines such as Boston ivy (*Parthenocissus tricuspidata*) and wintercreeper (*Euonymus fortunei*) tolerate dry shade, as do many perennials, such as bleeding hearts (*Dicentra*), stinking gladwyn (*Iris foetidisima*), comfrey (*Symphytum grandiflorum*), myrtle (*Vinca minor*), variegated bishop's weed (*Aegopodium podagraria* 'Variegata'), epimediums, ajugas, and bergenias.

### Alkaline soils

I have always loved the characteristic flora of alkaline soils, and many beautiful perennials, such as pasque flowers (*Pulsatilla vulgaris*), lily turfs (*Liriope*), hostas, and hellebores grow well in such conditions. Many culinary herbs also are suitable for alkaline conditions. Limestone base soils and rocks are found throughout Asia, as well as in the mountains of southern Europe, and in the

United States. A wide range of shrubs, trees, and vines grow in alkaline soils, including clematis, bottlebrush buckeye (*Aesculus parviflora*), lead plant (*Amorpha canescens*), butterfly bush (*Buddleia alternifolia*), redbuds (*Cercis*), oaks (*Quercus*), cotoneasters, forsythias, and spiraeas.

### Acidic soils

Gardens on a base acidic rock, such as granite, or under deciduous trees in areas with high rainfall, have acidic soils that support a diverse flora—not only a truly vast range of rhododendrons, azaleas, heaths, and heathers but also many members of the lily family, most gentians, and some splendid shrubs such as mountain laurels (*Kalmia*), blueberries (*Vaccinium*), *Pieris japonica*, *Clethra alnifolia*, *Itea virginica*, and *Leucothoe fontanesiana*. Dry, acidic soils are sometimes perceived as a problem but even here many plants do well, including brooms (*Cytisus*), sun roses (*Cistus*), *Tamarix*, and *Rosa rugosa*.

*Below* **The lesser periwinkle (*Vinca minor*) is one of the nicest species in a very useful genus. It will tuck itself into dark, dry corners and, once established, make a lovely glossy-leaved mat sparkling with small flowers—this is the white form, *Vinca minor* f. *alba*.**

# Precautionary principles

It is inconceivable that one or two individual gardeners can be held responsible for the rampaging colonization of alien plants over an important natural habitat, following the introduction of new species. In every case where this has happened, to my knowledge, it has taken widespread introduction into gardens, or even officially sanctioned introductions into the wild on a large scale that have unfortunately got out of hand. For example, mesembryanthemum, or ice plant (*Caprobrotus edule*), was planted to stabilize Californian road cuts, but then began to encroach severely on native sand dunes and coastal scrub vegetation. The common aquatic plant, water hyacinth (*Eichhornia crassipes*), indigenous to tropical America, was introduced as an ornamental to water systems but spread to choke waterways in many parts of the world. In Indonesia, it has, however, begun to be harvested as a food for pigs.

Himalayan balsam (*Impatiens balsamifera*) was introduced as a garden plant, naturalized readily in North America and Europe, and became an aggressive colonizer along slow-moving waterways

*Below* **The beautiful waving plumes of miscanthus grass —here growing respectably with teasel (*Dipsacus*) and neat conifers—may be a problem for the future. In hot, dry regions of the United States it is beginning to self-seed outside gardens in open countryside, and there are fears that it may overwhelm native plants.**

in Britain. Fortunately, the vigor of this plant seems now to be lessening, although population dynamics of naturalized weeds are imperfectly understood.

Plants that run riot are usually fairly reticent in their native regions. The beautiful scented *Rosa eglanteria* is not especially common in its native Europe, nor in its naturalized sites in North America, but it is a terrible nuisance in New Zealand, as is the Eurasian native clematis "old man's beard" (*Clematis vitalba*). The pretty Eurasian waterside plant, purple loosestrife (*Lythrum salicaria*), has recently become a problem in wetlands throughout much of North America.

## Localized problems

Sometimes a plant can become a nuisance locally, as the journalist Eleanor Perényi found when the attractive star of Bethlehem (*Ornithogalum umbellatum*) took over the lawn of her garden in Stonington, Connecticut. This plant is native to lowland Europe and has naturalized unobtrusively in parts of England. Chincherinchee (*O. thrysoides*), from South Africa, is a garden ornamental that

ventures timidly beyond the garden in some places, but is resented as a noxious weed in southern Australia. The flora and fauna of Australia and New Zealand are particularly vulnerable to aliens, but the fast-growing eucalyptus trees have exacted vengeance in southern and East Africa, the Mediterranean, Sri Lanka, and California.

## Gardening guidelines

Naturalization is never straightforward, however. The many species of eucalyptus trees that dominate parts of the California landscape, and which are the despair of conservationists concerned for the native ecology, have interwoven themselves into the ecological fabric in parts of Big Sur. Opposition to a eradication program has come from the local historical society, because of the age and size of some of the trees; from biologists concerned for the monarch butterflies, that use the eucalyptus as a roost as they migrate down the coast; and also from ornithologists, who appreciate the value of the flowers to orioles.

The precarious flora of this area of California coastline is also colonized by several weedy species of pampas grass (*Cortaderia atacamensis*)—considered by many to pose the most serious threat of all. Once established, it is difficult to eradicate, and many residents of the region are still

unwittingly planting it in their gardens, from where the seeds blow out into the wild. Another cause of this plant's spread is termed the "honeymoon dispersal mechanism," in recognition of the fashion among newlyweds of attaching a pampas plume to the radio aerials of their cars.

There are no precise rules governing the naturalization of plants. Some have grown strongly in gardens for centuries and never hop over the fence; others make a break during periods of social, horticultural, or climatic change; while for others there is no satisfactory explanation as yet for their behavior. It is, however, possible to outline a sensible code of practice for gardeners.

It is actually illegal to import or plant certain species in various places throughout the world, although being in touch with a local wildlife center would raise awareness in a neighborhood or region well before legislation was enacted and might help to halt the spread. In the case of water plants, it is particularly important never to dump surplus plants into the local waterways; much better to put them on to the compost pile, where they can be recycled back into the garden without causing harm.

Keeping a wary eye on changes in your local landscape and reporting unusual changes in plant life can also help regional ecologists to be kept informed on the overall state of the flora.

*Above left* **Mile-a-minute (*Fallopia baldschuanica*) grows prodigiously, although, as yet, it shows no sign of becoming rampant in the countryside. Plants in the wild are widespread but scattered, almost always taking root from discarded garden specimens or on the sites of derelict gardens.**

*Above right* **Purple loosestrife (*Lythrum salicaria*) looks marvelous here in a mixed poolside planting; in the United States, however, it has naturalized so vigorously that conservationists are worried that it is out-competing native lakeside and marshland species.**

# Boundaries

Although the grand landscape style appears to merge individual property with the wider landscape, in fact it only conceals the legal boundaries of property and land use that are everywhere strictly delineated. Gardens require definition, and smaller gardens, where properties abut, need clear boundaries. This need not entail conformism; there are many ways of marking boundary, both living and inorganic.

Walls are usually best made of local materials. If you inherit an ugly wall, you can probably clothe it in flower and foliage within a short period, thus turning an eyesore into an asset.

Fencing can be constructed in a vast number of materials and styles. For a natural effect, examine the styles of fences and gates in your region and search out something that appeals to you. Distinct styles of gate, for example, identify specific

localities. The United States takes a pride in its fence styles: split oak and chestnut were used for the zigzag Virginian rail fence, and hickory or locust tree in Pennsylvanian post and rail, while in Wyoming mitered buck fencing was constructed from local saplings. Although mass production dominates nowadays, you may still find a craft style or a way of doing things that gives a local signature.

## Hedges

Hedges give gardens both a sense of secure enclosure and natural order. They can also open to disclose a view or close off an unsightly prospect. Hedge plants that grow naturally large—privets, beeches, boxwoods, hawthorns, hornbeams, and yews, for example—may be clipped to control their size. Left to itself, a hedge naturally gains other species of plants. My own late-nineteenth-century

*Below* **An informal hedge of** *Rosa rugosa* **is hardy, windproof, and fragrant in summer. The semidouble, pink-flowered variety 'Belle Poitevine' has rich, bushy foliage and so is excellent for hedging. It is also highly scented and will thrive in poor soils.**

hedges, originally pure hawthorn, have now accrued wild rose, field maple, hazel, holly, and oak, as well as ivy and honeysuckle. I find that I need to trim them only twice a year.

Informal hedges take up more room but can be mysterious and relaxing. Rugosa roses and species shrub roses are ideal for informal hedges, together with species such as smoke tree (*Cotinus coggygria*), eleagnus (*Eleagnus angustifolia*), viburnums (*Viburnum lantana*), and cornelian cherry (*Cornus mas*). These may be planted in loose groupings or as a mixture of shrubs. One of the most effective is a hedge that starts off with three or four species planted slightly unevenly rather than in a straight line, which allows the shrubs to reach more or less their natural heights and spreads.

Using different varieties of a single species such as *Rosa rugosa* is better for smaller hedges. Its rich foliage and the scented flowers make this one of the most beautiful of all hedging plants. Planting in strict sequence will, however, create an undesirable formality, so dot colors here and there.

While hedge plants are getting their roots established and filling out, you may need to put in fencing to create a temporary boundary. This will also have the effect of providing some shelter to the shrubs as they mature.

A prickly, spiny hedge is an underappreciated yet effective deterrent for burglars. Ferocious hedging plants include holly (*Ilex*), pyracantha, barberries (*Berberis*), mahonia, and hawthorns (*Crataegus*), although you could choose anything that grows well locally provided it also produces unwelcoming prickles and spines.

## Internal divisions

As well as giving definition to the boundaries of your property, internal divisions may also be used to redefine certain areas within the garden. Sometimes dividing a garden a little can create an impression of greater space, although excessive subdivisions are more for a garden that has a formal rather than informal natural character.

You may, for example, choose a hedge to separate a wildflower orchard from an herb garden, perhaps clipping it lower than the outer boundary hedge, while at the same time indicating a clear division. You can use something as simple as a swathe of close-mown grass to separate an area of longer grass from a pathway or rough lawn. A line of espaliered trees makes a living trellis that suitably separates off a vegetable- or fruit-growing area.

Walls may also be built inside the garden, but they need to be used judiciously, as too much hardware will defeat a natural appearance. You can certainly have fun, however, planning where to cut gaps, gateways, archways, or vistas through them.

*Above* **A romantic end to a country garden, with a gate nestling under a tree on either side. The picket gate marks a definite boundary and allows not only a view to the outside but also evening sunlight to filter through.**

# CREATING A
## NATURAL GARDEN

Making and developing a garden in a natural style is a most creative and pleasurable activity, because it involves plants being situated in harmony with their surroundings and the flow of natural life. Go at your own pace; planning your own garden calls for understanding and clarity rather than speed. Even small changes make themselves felt within the larger scheme, and you can gradually build up the composition of the different habitats until you reach a balance that pleases you. This part of the book looks at a wide range of garden habitats and suggests ways for you to develop them.

*Left* There are few flowers more beautiful or so indicative of ancient woodland than the wood anemone. In this garden scene the carpet of natural white flowers has been augmented by a small drift of a pink variety.

*fter the dormancy of winter, the freshness and beauty of the early flora of deciduous woodland is one of the glories of the temperate world. In North American native forests, there are early phloxes, false Solomon's seal (Smilacina racemosa), and dogtooth violets (Erythronium), while in European forests wild daffodils (Narcissus pseudonarcissus), English bluebells (Hyacinthoides non-scripta), and wood anemones (Anemone nemorosa) abound.*

*Opposite* **For a shaded part of the garden, where a woodland-edge habitat can be created, the fresh foliage of the male fern (*Dryopteris filix-mas*) and the hart's tongue fern (*Asplenium scolopendrium*), growing through the purple-tinged low shoots of a bramble (*Rubus*), strike exactly the right note to the setting.**

# Beneath the trees

A planting under trees needs taste and restraint, because woodlands, more than any other habitat begin to look artificial if they become overcrowded. You should therefore choose a few species that do well and encourage self-seeding.

Why not take your cue for the woodland habitat of the garden by studying the edges of woods and path sides, where more light falls than in the denser interior canopy and where a succession of flowers will bloom throughout summer and the fall. The design approach and the kinds and number of species you choose will depend on the size of your garden as well as the scope of your ambition.

At the very minimum you will be able to grow snowdrops (*Galanthus nivalis*) or winter aconite (*Eranthis hyemalis*), dame's rocket (*Hesperis matronalis*), and honesty (*Lunaria annua*) along the shady base of a hedge or wall.

Many people wrongly perceive shade as a disadvantage. Some of the most subtle and successful effects in the garden can be created within shady borders. As this habitat supports a particularly wide range of plants, there is no shortage of choice, even in early summer. You could try lily of the valley (*Convallaria*), foam flowers (*Tiarella*), hostas, and arching Solomon's seal (*Polygonatum biflorum*), all of which grow well even in quite dense shade.

Woodland-edge soil is usually rich and quite fertile. Shade-loving woodland plants therefore do much better in such conditions than, for example, herbs. If the area you have in mind for a woodland edge has poor soil, plant foxgloves (*Digitalis*), red catchfly (*Silene dioica*), foamflowers (*Tiarella cordifolia*), cyclamen (*Cyclamen coum* or *C. hederifolium*), and hellebores as first colonizers, while you build up fertility by adding compost.

*Left* **Early spring flowers such as common snowdrops (*Galanthus nivalis*), winter aconites (*Eranthus hyemalis*), and early-flowering hellebores will withstand snow and late frost. These plants look best under deciduous shrubs and trees, such as this Indian plum (*Oemleria cerasiformis*).**

# Woodland flora in the garden

The area in most gardens where shade is dominant is usually the best place to start with woodland flora. The transformation to a more natural style, however, should flow gently, with additional plants in the new design gradually being absorbed.

In wild conditions, the flower-rich edge of woodland merges imperceptibly into deep forest. As this is unlikely to occur in the garden, you need a distinct framework, perhaps that of the garden boundary itself. If your garden lies on an east-west axis, there is the opportunity for a north-facing woodland-edge border that can be a pure delight. A longish border between a path and a boundary hedge, for example, can have a number of phases, punctuated by taller plants. Such phasing could also be practised in a rectangular or irregular area, such as at the bottom of the garden or in an alcove.

When working with a fairly long border, I like to create a sense of pace by interrupting the high border plants with a small grassy area, perhaps with a small tree to give the impression of a linear woodland walk. A group of snowdrops (*Galanthus*), dogtooth violets (*Erythronium*), or autumn crocus (*Colchicum*), planted in the grass, continues the woodland theme but allows for mowing through most of the year, after the bulbs have died back.

Snowdrops and dogtooth violets (*Erythronium*) do equally well in beds and borders, along with other very easily established winter-into-spring plants such as cyclamen. Two mainstays are the dainty *Cyclamen hederifolium* and *C. coum* (flowering in autumn and winter respectively), which give delightful silver-on-dark-green leaf patterning, as well as attractive pink flowers blotched deep carmine at the mouth. Both species have attractive white forms.

Violets, such as the scented *Viola odorata*, which flowers in spring, and the purplish-leaved *V. labradorica*, which flowers slightly later from spring into early summer, are hardy and easy to establish, while the elegant pale blue *V. cornuta* has been widely adopted as a garden plant. Other good wild violets to consider include the scented Canada violet (*V. canadensis*) and cream-colored *V. striata*. A patch of *V. cornuta* looks lovely, but all violets make a valuable contribution, whether planted in groups, in twos or threes, or individually. The idea in this habitat is to make a rich patchwork of woodland species. This could also include wood anemone, Virginia bluebells (*Mertensia virginica*), Jacob's ladder (*Polemonium*), wild blue phlox (*Phlox divaricata*), and bleeding hearts (*Dicentra eximia* and *D. formosa*).

The exquisite dogtooth violets, also called trout lilies, are neither violets nor lilies but *Erythronium* species. Although fragile looking, they will naturalize quite readily in suitable soils. They are subtle plants and look best when planted in small groups, offset against a background of ferns or foliage that show up the full beauty of their decorative, spotted, glossy leaves and flowers with thrown-back petals.

Brilliant drifts of spring color give place to pale, glimmering blooms that light up the summer shade. Several hardy geraniums thrive in these conditions. The spotted geranium (*Geranium macrorrhizum*), with its scented leaves, makes an attractive rounded hump of foliage when not flowering. The dusky cranesbill (*G. phaeum*) and

*Below* **Autumn crocuses (*Colchicum autumnale*) growing in turf. There are fancier varieties, but in a naturalistic planting this species looks superb.**

*Bottom* **Forget-me-nots line the path to this woodland, presided over by fine foxgloves (*Digitalis purpurea*). Foamflowers (*Tiarella cordifolia*) can be seen in the foreground.**

the white form of the common herb Robert
(*G. robertianum*), which will lighten a dark corner,
both self-seed readily. The attractive *G. maculatum*
grows best in drifts in moist dappled shade, and
*G. sylvaticum* will survive trying conditions. These
geraniums look good grown with taller summer
plants, such as foxgloves (*Digitalis purpurea*). The
pure white form looks startling growing in shaded
conditions but both pink and white forms self-seed
naturally and dot themselves about. Also tallish and
clumping, astilbes and masterwort (*Astrantia major*)
shine in the late summer, and the Chinese anemone
(*Anemone hupehensis*) is a treasure that, once
established, will flower and increase reliably.

## PLANTING PLAN FOR A WOODLAND EDGE

The shaded environment beneath trees can be one of the most beautiful in
a garden. Soil that is initially dry and poor can be improved naturally with
the introduction of thoroughly rotted organic compost and leaf mold (a
quick route to the rich buildup of humus that occurs in a natural
woodland). Woodland plants in this dappled woodland-edge situation
bloom well over a long period of the growing season.

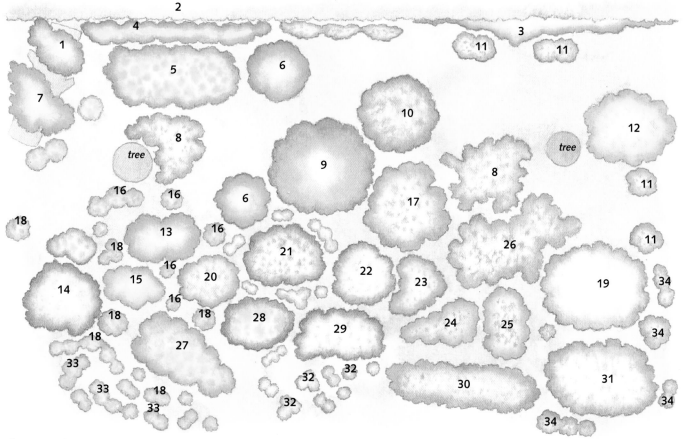

*key to planting*

1  Ivy *Hedera helix*
2  Beech hedge *Fagus syslvatica*
3  *Clematis montana*
4  Comfrey *Symphytum grandiflorum*
5  Yellow loosestrife *Lysimachia vulgaris*
6  Male fern *Dryopteris filix-mas*
7  Virginia creeper *Parthenocissus quinquefolia*
8  *Cyclamen hederifolium*
9  Smoke tree *Cotinus* 'Grace'
10  Fennel *Foeniculum vulgare* 'Purpureum'
11  Honesty *Lunaria annua*
12  *Geranium macrorrhizum*

13  Hart's-tongue fern *Asplenium scholopenrium*
14  *Rubus* 'Benenden'
15  *Tolmeia menziessi* 'Taff's Gold'
16  Welsh poppy *Meconopsis cambrica*
17  Foxglove *Digitalis purpurea*
18  Daffodils *Narcissus pseudonarcissus* 'Tête-à-tête'
19  Bowman's root *Gillenia trifoliata*
20  *Geranium sylvaticum*
21  *Geranium phaeum*
22  Snowy woodrush *Luzula nivea*
23  Sweet woodruff *Galium odoratum*

24  *Cardamine pentaphyllum*
25  Shooting star *Dodecatheon pulchellum*
26  English bluebell *Hyacinthoides hispanica*
27  Lady's mantle *Alchemilla mollis*
28  Dogtooth violet/Trout lily *Erythronium revolutum*
29  *Lamium* 'White Nancy'
30  Bugleweed *Ajuga reptans* 'Atropurpurea'
31  *Brunnera macrophylla*
32  Snowdrop *Galanthus nivalis*
33  Winter aconite *Eranthis hyemalis*
34  Wild blue phlox *Phlox divaricata*

# Shrubs and vines

The woodland edge is a place where shrubs thrive because more light is available, in contrast to the inner heartland of the forest. The garden counterpart has immense possibilities, and indeed one has to hold back from the temptation to plant too many shrubs (especially when they are young and small). Placing shrubs at intervals to suit the spirit of your design, giving a flow in terms of color and texture, however, makes a desirable change of pace. When planning an area, I look first at the native shrubs of a region, then at other shrubs that perform particularly well in shade and for which I have a preference, and gradually fine-tune a personal choice down to those that would suit that particular piece of woodland garden.

Shrubs are particularly useful in punctuating a long, shady border. I originally picked out *Rubus* 'Benenden' for its large white flowers, which come in spring, but was pleased to find the foliage turns a beautiful amber in late summer. Viburnums have a huge geographical range and make a pleasing ingredient to a woodland-edge border, especially if you can key in the species with those that grow naturally in the surrounding landscape. Wayfaring tree (*Viburnum lantana*) grows along the roadsides near woods where I live, and I chose the similar-looking *V. carlesii* 'Diana,' which has compact growth and richly-scented spring flowers. If my border merged into grass rather than a path, I would have planted the European snowball (*Viburnum opulus*) in the dappled shade, for its beautiful glossy leaves, white lacecap flowers, and glorious red berries. There must be a viburnum for nearly every situation, but it is important in natural gardening to choose a kind that fits with both the garden location and the woodland theme.

Bowman's root, or Indian physic (*Gillenia trifoliata*), is an unusual shrub that rewards close inspection. It has dark, bronzy foliage, three-lobed leaves growing on red-brown twigs, and bears, over a long season, irregular white blossoms, dainty and brilliant, that seem to float against the darker background. Bowman's root grows naturally along roadsides near upland woods over a wide area of North America. It takes readily to woodland-edge borders in light shade and also tolerates acid to slightly alkaline soil.

Large shrubs with open foliage, such as oakleaf hydrangea (*Hydrangea quercifolia*), look good judiciously placed in larger woodland gardens. However, in general, I feel the large, showy exotics such as hydrangeas or rhododendrons should be used with extreme caution. Sometimes, however, flora from far afield works very well together with native plants. Happy associations may come about almost accidentally. An instance of this happened in my woodland-edge border, when I decided to plant a bush of *Cotinus* 'Grace,' which has large purple-tinged leaves. Behind it, a self-seeded fennel sprang up, and to the side a tree peony (*P. delavayii*), which has rather beautiful cut-leaved foliage and deep crimson flowers, was beginning to fill out. In between, a self-seeded dark purple *Geranium phaeum* and chocolate-colored columbines (*Aquilegia vulgaris*) made this one of the most attractive parts of the shady wood-edge border, even though it had occurred almost by chance.

*Below* **Witch hazels (*Hamamelis*) bring their bright, wispy flowers and strong scent to late winter and early spring. Lemon-colored 'Sunburst' grows here with the cultivar 'Diane,' which has coppery-colored flowers. Both bloom from mid- to late winter and require neutral to acidic soil conditions to grow well.**

Although golden-foliaged plants look extremely unnatural, some plants have a golden glow that is not so flashy and is just what is needed in shady conditions. A perennial I would include in this select group is golden piggyback plant (*Tolmiea menziesii* 'Taff's Gold'). It is low growing and undemanding, with handsome soft foliage speckled with gold. It spreads quietly to make a golden pool of color. New plants form on top of the leaves where the old leaf meets the leaf stalk. Bolder and more showy, *Hosta* 'Midas Gold' is a golden form that does well in shade, while the discreet golden form of creeping Jenny (*Lysimachia nummularia* 'Aurea') will run prettily under trees and shrubs in light to medium shade. I am tempted also by *Rubus idaeus* 'Aureus,' which tolerates lightly shaded conditions. Place the golden plants sparingly, and separate them by others with darker foliage. Allow the yellow or golden forms of the Welsh poppy (*Mecanopsis cambrica*) to self-seed, and any prejudice you may have held against these sometimes-garish plants will be replaced with real appreciation.

## Climbing plants

Well-chosen vines bring an airy lightness of flower to the trees or hedges they drape, and lead the eye upward. They can be combined with shrubs in a woodland-edge context: I look out on to my woodland border through a window framed with Mexican orange blossom (*Choisya ternata*) on one

*Above* Mock orange (*Philadelphus*) makes a lovely garden shrub, with its rich scent and white flowers. There are single- and double-flowered cultivars. 'Belle Etoile,' with a crimson dab at each flower center, is one of the most popular singles. Seen here in the company of yellow loosestrife (*Lysimachia punctata*), mock oranges flower in early summer.

side and the partly evergreen, winter-fragrant honeysuckle (*Lonicera fragrantissima*) on the other. Honeysuckle is a natural inhabitant of woods and woodland edge and has an incomparable scent that is an important constituent of a summer evening. The English would say that the woodbine (*L. periclymenum*) has the best scent, but whether the trumpets are pollinated by hummingbirds or bumblebees, they are welcome in gardens (with the exception of *L. japonica*, an Asian species, which has become a serious weed in North America).

*Clematis montana* is a vigorous vine that, unlike most clematis, enjoys a woodland situation and will happily romp up trees and over hedges or stumps, producing masses of small, slightly scented flowers. *C.m. wilsonii* and 'Odorata,' both white-flowered kinds, are particularly strongly scented, bringing a delicious sweet vanilla to the early summer wood garden. These clematis do not require pruning and are hardy and generally trouble-free.

In recent years, an increasing number of named cultivars of *C. montana* have become generally available. 'Warwickshire Rose' and 'Mayleen,' for example, have satin-pink flowers against bronze foliage and are strongly vanilla scented. Pink forms need to be used with care so as not to look artificial in the woodland garden. They look good alongside paths and are a very handsome and a splendid covering of large boundary walls, growing high into a tree or bringing a light touch to a large, heavy conifer. *C. montana* is reliably hardy in zones 6–9, but is not yet as well known as it deserves to be.

There are a vast number of ivy cultivars, some of them very fussy and artificial-looking and therefore best kept well away from the woodland-edge garden, where the accent is on a natural effect. Choose instead one of the glossy, dark green ivies that are closer to the species, such as *Hedera helix* 'Hibernica' or perhaps 'Deltoidea.'

*Opposite* **Summer-flowering honeysuckle (*Lonicera periclymenum*) is among the most beautiful and sweetest-smelling plants. It is traditionally planted around doorways so that the scent can be enjoyed to the fullest; it is at its best on walls and fences or over dead trees.**

Many small-leaved sports of the common English ivy look good in a small garden. Some, such as 'Glacier', are attractively variegated and can lighten a dark corner. 'Green Ripple,' as the name implies, has a leaf that looks as if it were under water. Ivies naturally grow up trees, and they will also cover bare ground, rooting from their stems.

The white climbing hydrangea (*Hydrangea anomala petiolaris*) is not uncommon in gardens, although it is not often grown up trees. It can look very attractive in this situation, because you have a clear view of the flowers and, in winter, of the handsome flaking cinnamon-colored bark of the trunk and twigs. It is self-clinging but appreciates a little support while it is getting established.

The golden hop (*Humulus lupulus* 'Aureus') is a vigorous and attractive plant that is eye-catching without appearing too garish when seen growing into a tree or large shrub. The crimson glory vine (*Vitis coignetiae*), usually grown over walls, can also be grown up the trunk of a large tree, making a dramatic swirl of foliage and giving an autumn color of fiery crimson and scarlet.

Roses, such as *Rosa* 'Complicata,' or one of the rambling varieties that are able to tolerate a degree of dryness and shade also make a lovely show growing up into a tree in a wood-edge situation.

*Below* **A beautifully toned combination of shrubs and vines: white *Clematis* 'Silver Moon' growing through blue-leaved *Rosa glauca*, with fluffy-flowered meadow rue (*Thalictrum aquilegifolium*) and *Clematis* 'Niobe' peeping through to the right.**

# Trees

A mature tree is a tremendous gift to a garden. Whatever else you plant will certainly fall short of the grandeur of a tree that has grown through several generations of human activity. Ryan Gainey, the American garden designer, moving to his garden in Decatur near Atlanta, Georgia, noted first "a beautiful white oak, a winged elm of good size, and a male American holly as my gardening companions." Beth Chatto, who set up a garden in the notoriously dry English county of Essex, argues forcibly that you should take out redundant plants that are well past their best, but have the sense to recognize "a rare antique"—in her case six old oaks that had formed part of a farm boundary. Both

these gardeners rose to the task and within a few years had created glorious and individual gardens that flourished beneath their fine old trees.

A large tree or group of mature trees presents an obvious starting place for a woodland-edge garden, using the shapes of the trees and the fall of the shade to guide the design. Having rid the ground of weeds, you need to dig, aerate, and mulch the compacted soil where you can, planting where possible into the most fertile patches.

If you are starting a new garden and have no trees, consider carefully which species to plant. Since most modern gardens are on a smaller scale than those of the past, it is a shame to plant a tree

*Below* **This beautiful white double-flowered flowering cherry has an unusually open and generous branching habit. The owners are still puzzling its precise identification but are delighted with its annual showing in early spring.**

that is inherently too large so that you have to top it or, even worse, take it out because it threatens roofs, windows, and drains. Do not forget that trees can also cause a nuisance by being too tall; Leyland and Lawson cypresses, planted as boundary trees in small gardens, continue to cause misery to light-starved owners and neighbors. There are plenty of beautiful small and medium-sized trees that bring unalloyed pleasure.

For a natural style of gardening, choose trees that are close to those native to the landscape or nonnatives that will fit in well. Trees, being larger, will make their presence felt more emphatically than ground-hugging plants, so avoid trees with violent or artificial coloring of flowers or foliage. Those such as oak and beech cast deep shade, while others such as ash and birch allow more light through to the ground below. You could choose trees for elegance of shape, for rapid (or slow) growth, or to provide ornamental or edible fruit.

*Left* Paper birch (*Betula papyrifera*) has pale bark that peels in thin layers. A tall tree, its leaves turn through yellow to golden-orange in autumn. Grown individually or in small groups, as here, they are seen to perfection in open ground.

## A GUIDE TO SELECTING TREES FOR YOUR GARDEN

### SMALL TREES

**Crabapples** *Malus* species
10–40ft (3–12m) • sweet-scented spring flowers, good autumn color, colorful fruit from summer to winter • any soil • sun– very light shade • fruit, especially of small-fruited cultivars, attracts birds and other wildlife • select disease-resistant cultivars

**Eastern redbud** *Cercis canadensis*
20–30ft (6–9m) • showy spring flowers, some yellow • fall color • any soil except permanently wet ones • full sun to partial shade • can be used as a specimen or planted along forest edges • white- and pink-flowered forms are available • 'Forest Pansy' has red-purple, spring foliage • Chinese redbud (*C. chinensis*) is a multistemmed shrub suitable for specimen use or shrub borders

**Blackhaw viburnum** *Viburnum prunifolium*
10–20ft (3–6m) • white spring flowers, black fall fruit, good fall color • any soil • sun or shade • can be used as a small tree or large shrub, as a specimen, or in shrub borders or hedges

### MEDIUM-SIZE TREES

**Korean mountain ash** *Sorbus alnifolia*
40–50ft (12–15m) • spring flowers, orange summer fruit, good autumn color • any well-drained soil • sun • does not tolerate pollution or heat, and best grown in zone 7 north

**Birch** *Betula platyphylla* 'Whitespire'
**River birch** *Betula nigra*
40–70ft (12–23m) • *B. platyphylla* 'Whitespire' has white bark • *B. nigra* has shaggy pink-brown bark • both are resistant to bronze birch bore • most soils • sun to partial shade • airy open trees, good in small clumps or single stemmed • *B nigra* 'Heritage' is an outstanding selection that is heat tolerant and has white-salmon bark on young branches, salmon-brown on older growth

**Black tupelo** *Nyssa sylvatica*
30–50ft (9–15m) • rich green leaves in summer • outstanding scarlet to purple, autumn foliage • moist, well-drained, slightly acidic soil • full sun or partial shade • can be difficult to transplant • black fall fruit is attractive to birds and mammals

### LARGER TREES

**Pin oak** *Quercus palustris*
**Red oak** *Quercus rubra*
60–70ft (18–21m) • many species of large spreading trees with acorns for wildlife and good autumn color • most soils, but acidic to neutral is best • bur oak (*Q. macrocarpa*) tolerates high pH soils • long-lived, beautiful trees • many species can be difficult to transplant, but *Q. palustris* is relatively easy

**Scotch pine** *Pinus sylvestris*
**Eastern white pine** *Pinus strobus*
30–60ft (9–18m) and over • most soils, but best in acidic to neutral pH • full sun • easily transplanted • *P. strobus* does not tolerate air pollution or salt

**Green ash** *Fraxinus pennsylvanica*
50–60ft (18–21m) • very adaptable tree for any soil, including alkaline, moist, and dry • full sun for best color and form • select a named cultivar • self-sowing can be a problem • 'Marshall's Seedless' is a nonfruiting, male form with good fall color

All plants need moisture, but while some are adapted to thrive in damp ground, relatively few can survive in waterlogged conditions. Only specialized aquatic plants live their entire life cycles submerged or semisubmerged. If you can discover or contrive a damp area or a pool in your garden, you create a site for a range of plants that is not only endlessly fascinating in itself but is also a habitat that invites a selection of fauna and flora of incredible intricacy and beauty.

*Opposite* **A luxuriant spring scene with yellow flag (*Iris pseudacorus*) and snakeweed (*Persicaria bistorta* 'Superba') flowering in the damp foreground, while gunnera (*Gunnera manicata*), skunk cabbage (*Lysichiton americanus*), and shrubs typical of marshy ground inhabit the edges and slightly higher ground in the background.**

# Water and wetland

Siting a bog garden or pool that will look natural in your garden entails exploring a wide range of possibilities. The means for making water features in gardens are now so sophisticated that you could make a pool, lake, or fountain just about anywhere, suitable or not. It is important not to be hasty but to make considered preparations, so that when you

finally start planting in or beside the water, it will immediately look absolutely natural. Even if you have to make an artificial construction, try to interfere as little as possible with natural cycles, aiming to integrate your water centerpiece in a way that is as self-sustaining as it can be.

Select a site that is within convenient reach of a hose. Once the pond is filled, rainwater will make up for much of the evaporation loss, but you will probably need to fill it up periodically, especially during hot, dry weather. If you want to incorporate a fountain or other feature with moving water, you will also need to run an electric cable to the site to provide power for a pump.

There are many different ways of introducing water into a garden: fountains, waterfalls, canals, or a simulated bogland. A pool surrounded by grass and plants is one of the easiest to fit into a natural garden. Once you have the pool, you may want to try a spout or pebble pool—water is addictive. The pleasure of the reflected plants, dragonflies, and other creatures that frequent the pool, plus the air of tranquillity that a pool brings to a garden, make the initial labors seem a very small cost compared to the deep and lasting pleasures.

*Left* **A damp spot area, populated by ferns, lady's mantle, and skunk cabbage; deep pink candelabra primroses (*Primula beesiana*) create an element of spring drama beside the fresh green foliage.**

# Wetland for the ordinary garden

Many gardens have a damp section in their yard, perhaps signaled by reeds, lush grass, or creeping buttercups. It is usually the part over which landscape gardeners will shake their heads and then suggest expensive systems of drainage that will ruin you and disrupt your existing garden. Surely it is better to take a cue from nature and look for plants that enjoy the moisture. Such damp-loving plants offer tremendous choice and will take you through from the early spring flush of marsh marigolds (*Caltha palustris*) to asters in the fall.

In the past, people understood how to use land just as it was. Among the best farm habitats were water meadows—low-lying lands that flooded in winter and grew a vast range of meadow flowers in spring and summer. A damp area of lawn will support creeping Jenny (*Lysimachia nummularia*), a trailing plant with bright yellow flowers. Bugleweed (*Ajuga reptans*) bears erect spikes of violet-blue flowers in spring and will compete nicely with lawn grass. Bronze-leaved and brightly variegated forms are available. Meadowsweet (*Filipendula ulmaria*) flies its tall creamy plumes in late summer and, topping that, queen of the prairies (*F. rubra*) makes a stunning clump of pink flowers on tall stems. Other U.S. native wildflowers that thrive in moist soil include turtleheads (*Chelone lyonii*).

The checkered lily (*Fritillaria meleagris*) is a native of meadows that flood in the winter months. It naturalizes well in gardens, including those that

*Above* A sure sign of damp ground, and a reliable performer for such areas, snakeweed (*Persicaria bistorta*) will naturalize freely. The native species is pale pink, *P. b.* subsp. *carnea* is a deeper pink, while 'Superba' has more rounded, pale pink flower heads.

*Left* This tranquil damp meadow in a grass ravine boasts a falling stream and red and white checkered fritillary (*Fritillaria meleagris*). The small curved bulbs of this fritillary are more likely to grow well if they are planted in summer, before they dry out.

are only slightly damp. The good-natured lady's mantle (*Alchemilla mollis*) will also naturalize in grass. There it makes a good foil to astilbes, which are native to moist places in mountain ravines, woodsides, and along stream banks in North America and Southeast Asia. The species *Astilbe chinensis* grows to about 2ft (60cm), bearing panicles of pink-white flowers in late summer, although you are more likely to encounter some of its many hybrids. *A. chinensis pumila*—to 10in (25cm)—has deep pink flowers. Popular *A. simplicifolia* 'Sprite' is taller—20in (50cm)—and forms a dense clump of narrow-leaved foliage with feathery pale pink flowers in summer. In reliably damp conditions, astilbes may be grown in sun or light shade, but in ground that may dry out in summer they prefer partial shade.

Sun-loving daylilies *(Hemerocallis)* like a moist but well-drained soil, and in their Asian homelands they grow in damp meadows and marshy river valleys. Having escaped from gardens, they have become widely naturalized and are often used in wild gardens, where they look best planted in drifts or groups. Tawny daylily (*Hemerocallis fulva*) has big orange-bronze flowers, while lemon daylily (*H. lilioasphodelus*) bears fragrant lemon-yellow flowers. Both clump up to a sturdy 3ft (1m) in height and diameter. Hybrid daylilies come in a wide range of colors and sizes. For a natural garden, old-fashioned hybrids, which have smaller, more classic-looking blooms, are most appropriate.

*Crocosmia* is usually found in flower borders, but it will thrive in any moist, humus-rich soil. I remember the brilliant red *C. masoniorum* from a clump that was almost the only plant surviving in a ruined garden, its bright flowers indicating where flower beds had once been. *C.* x *crocosmiiflora*, a hybrid between *C. aurea* and *C. pottsii*, was first raised in France in 1880. It and 'Citronella' and 'Emily McKenzie' are only hardy in zones 6–9.

*Above* **Astilbes, with their graceful feathery flower heads, male fern (*Dryopteris filix-mas*), and royal fern (*Osmunda regalis*) make handsome complementary partners. Smaller hybrid astilbes are now available, so they can be grown in even a small marshy or pondside area.**

## Wetland trees and shrubs

Trees that are suited to damp places include willows (*Salix*), poplars (*Populus*), the glorious sweet gum (*Liquidamber styraciflua*), and bald cypress (*Taxodium distichum*). Red maple (*Acer rubrum*) thrives in damp soil. It bears clouds of tiny red flowers in very early spring before the leaves emerge. In fall, its foliage turns brilliant red.

Sycamores, or plane trees (*Platanus*), are fine choices for wet spots, since they grow naturally along rivers and streams. American plane tree (*P. occidentalis*) and London plane tree (*P. x acerifolia*) both feature handsome exfoliating bark. Sweet bay (*Magnolia virginiana*), which is evergreen in the southern United States and deciduous in the north, bears fragrant white flowers in early summer followed by showy red fruit. It will thrive in damp and even swampy soil.

Many attractive shrubs also enjoy damp conditions. Among the most spectacular for winter interest are the red-stemmed Tatarian dogwood (*Cornus alba*) and redosier dogwood (*C. sericea*). *C. sericea* 'Cardinal' has cherry red stems in winter, while 'Flaviramea' has yellow ones. The young stems are most colorful, so cut one third of the older stems to the ground each spring. Hydrangeas of many kinds thrive in shady, damp places. Among some of the larger bushy herbaceous perennials, rodgersias (*Rodgersia*), goatsbeard (*Aruncus dioicus*), *Darmera peltata*, and Chinese rhubarb (*Rheum palmatum*) make very handsome damp-ground plants.

## Dips and ditches

Having a natural stream in your garden must be the greatest joy, and I unashamedly envy people who possess this feature. The nearest I have ever come to having one was a shady drainage ditch attached to the end of a small, dry, alkaline garden, where in the winter months and sometimes during the summer a small stream would run. Initially, it had little or no vegetation, but planted with woodland plants it became very pretty.

I have seen larger damp ditches, improved by the addition of leaf mold, transformed into a home for primroses, ferns, hellebores, dicentras, woodland euphorbias, and gentians. One side of the ditch will typically get more sun, while the other can be a home to shade-loving plants.

Many handsome and compact plants, such as foamflowers (*Tiarella cordifolia*) and lungworts (*Pulmonaria*), grow well in damp dips and ditches, as does coral bells (*Heuchera*). All of these plants have foliage of particular beauty, so that they look just as attractive out of flower. Hostas come in large and small sizes, with a variety of leaf textures and patterns. These plants are grown principally for their foliage, but they also have very pretty flowers. If you have room for a really big fern, try the unusual royal fern (*Osmunda regalis*), which makes a big clumpy plant that can grow to 6ft (2m), with large, bright green pinnate fronds.

*Below* **This quiet rill under a retaining wall creates humidity for mosses, ferns, and bog plants. Hardy geraniums as well as wild strawberries (*Fragaria vesca*) cascade on the bank, and clumps of Siberian iris (*Iris sibirica*) and tender calla lilies (*Zantedeschia*) backed by mulleins (*Verbascum*), lines the opposite side.**

## Swampy ground

Even perpetually swampy ground will support plants that give a range of flowers, foliage, and textures throughout the year. Marsh marigolds (*Caltha palustris*) make a wonderful bright gold start to the year, while deliciously scented water mint (*Mentha aquatica*) and bog arum, or yellow skunk cabbage (*Lysichitum americanus*), are ready colonizers that will need controlling in sites where they are happy. Any water mint that transgresses into a pond can be easily lifted out, while a quick way to control stems that stray into the drier parts of the lawn is simply to mow them.

A number of waterside irises will thrive in boggy ground, including *Iris laevigata* and its variegated version, where the purple-blue flowers are almost hidden in the handsome ivory and green leaves.

Yellow flag (*Iris pseudacorus*) will grow in marshy ground as well as standing water, as will two irises native to the United States, Southern blue flag (*I. virginica*) and blue flag (*I. versicolor*). Gardeners in warmer regions (zones 6–11) should also consider some of the stunning Louisiana irises. Lady's mantle (*Alchemilla*) is another surprisingly adaptable plant, tolerating wet conditions as well as drought. I have seen this plant providing an excellent link between some more colorful species in a large bog garden traversed by stepping stones of local rock.

If you have to create wetland artificially, the plants around a pool or fountain will be affected by the humidity arising from the water. Keep in mind that if you use a liner to construct your bog or water garden, the soil surrounding it will be no wetter than the rest of your garden's soil.

*Above* A sensational combination of *Iris ensata* cultivars, grown with variegated grass (*Phalaris arundinacea picta*) and the white *Zantedeschia aethiopica* 'Crowborough.' This long-flowering plant needs moist rich soil and sun and is hardy to zone 8 if mulched in winter.

# Water plants and bog plants

A natural style of pool or pond calls for plants growing in the water and around the edges. The skill lies in suiting the plants to the scale of the area of water and making a composition that looks as natural as possible. A number of water plants are vigorous in growth, and it is helpful to look at estimated mature size before planting. There are so many good plants it is difficult to resist overplanting, but the effect is usually better if you allow gaps on the banks.

The most common problem with ponds is usually an overabundance of algae, which makes the water turn green. This is most likely to occur in a new pond or an early, sunny spring. The cause is an excess of nutrients in the water, which is not yet being used by the submerged oxygenating plants, because they take a little longer to begin growing than the algae. Since free-floating algae require sunlight to grow, shading the pool helps prevent them from reproducing. Surface-floating plants

## PLANTING BOG PLANTS AND AQUATICS

**Silver willow**
*Salix alba sericea*
Fast-growing upright tree with silver-gray leaves. Prune hard to keep size down and for fresh stems.

**Water mint**
*Mentha aquatica*
Grows in water or as a bog plant; vigorous; lavender-blue flowers in summer, scented leaves.

**River birch**
*Betula nigra*
Dark leaves, spring catkins, attractive peeling red-brown bark; tall (60ft/18m) when mature.

**Soft rush**
*Juncus effusus*
Common and easily established bog species. Dark green, stiff grasslike foliage.

**Alder** *Alnus glutinosa*
Good bog tree; early spring catkins, rich dark foliage, small dark fruits enjoyed by seed-eating birds.

**Silver birch**
*Betula pendula*
Elegant tree; silver-white barked, early spring catkins, small diamond-shaped leaves.

*Iris laevigata*
Stately blue-flowered iris; blooms in early summer in bog or shallow water; good variegated form.

such as duckweed or fairy moss (*Azolla filiculoides*) are an easy option for smaller ponds. Floating plants and water lilies shade the water and prevent algae from forming, and also keep the water from overheating during the summer. Keep 60–70 percent of the water surface covered with plants—scoop out excess surface-floating plants and add them to the compost pile. The water in your pool may still "green up" in spring, but be patient. As soon as the plants resume growing, it will clear up. Avoid using chemical treatments.

*Right* **Pickerel weed (*Pontederia cordata*) is a vigorous aquatic and bog plant. The tawny-orange daylilies behind need damp soil and plenty of hot sun, in order to flower as profusely as this, while the yellow *Lysimachia* behind prefers to grow in a little shade.**

**Cattails**
*Typha latifolia*
Pond and pool edges; dark brown flower heads. Sun or shade; vigorous growth.

**Yellow flag**
*Iris pseudacorus*
Grows in moist soil or shallow water; yellow flowers in late spring. Vigorous growth.

**Fringed water lily**
*Nymphoides peltata*
Clear yellow-fringed flowers above small heart-shaped leaves in summer.

**Water soldier**
*Stratiotes aloides*
Aquatic floating perennial in a leafy rosette of narrow leaves that sinks to the bottom in autumn.

**Bogbean**
*Menyanthes trifoliata*
Bog plant with pretty three-lobed leaves and fringed pale pink flowers.

**Pickerel weed**
*Pontaderia cordata*
Glossy lance-shaped leaves; rich blue flower spikes bloom in summer and the fall.

**Hornwort** *Ceratophyllum demersum* Submerged aquatic oxygenator with finely forked leaves; sinks to the bottom in winter.

# A natural-style pond

It is important when siting a garden pond to make the right preparations so that by the time you start planting in or beside the water, it will look absolutely natural. If you want birds and other wildlife to be able to visit your pond to drink, plan on using a flexible liner. Preformed fiberglass pools have steep sides and prevent creatures from having access to the water.

After you have decided on the right place for the pond, start by laying out the shape with pegs and hose. Keep in mind that ponds that have at least one deeper part (about 3ft/1m) tend to be easier to manage and are better at self-regulation. It is conventional to create a shallower outer shelf, stepping down to a deeper part. If you intend to keep your plants in perforated pots, this gives them something to stand on.

When you are satisfied with the shape and dimensions, you can begin to dig out the hole. This should be about 6in (15cm) deeper than the final depth to allow for the space taken up by the insulation and liner. If you intend to have a pump, you will also need to create a channel to the edge of the pond for the cable (and protective plastic conduit). Cut a 6in (15cm) lip all around the perimeter of the pond to lay the overlap liner

on. If you want a small swampy area next to the pond, extend this lip to make a bowl shape that can be refilled with soil later. Use the topsoil elsewhere in the garden and dispose of the dank subsoil.

The best liners are made from butyl or EPDM (ethylene propylene diene monomer), since these are tough enough to last about fifty years. Your supplier will be able to help you calculate the amount of waterproof liner required. Before you put your liner in place, pick out any sharp objects and lay a 2in (5cm) layer of moist sand. Gardens with clay soil, or clay and flint, should also cushion the liner with a brand-name underlay. Position the underlay carefully and then the liner, so that it fits smoothly and without stretching, molding to the form of the pond (and bog area if you have one). For best effect, fit some overlay on top of the liner to protect it from direct sunlight and also to provide a nonslippery base for a soil layer. Then gently add a soil layer, and one of gravel if you want. The optional gravel helps keep the soil layer in place.

When filling the pond, do not run a hose directly into it or you will create a cloud of mud. Instead, place the hose on some underlay so that the water filters in slowly, gradually amplifying until the required water depth is reached.

**MAKING A POND**

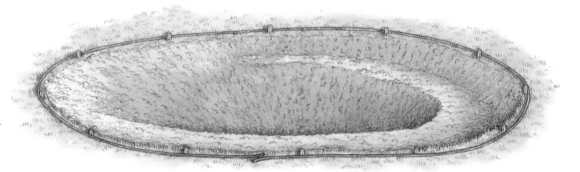

1 Dig out the pond, keeping just inside the designated boundary. Remove rocks and anything else that might puncture the liner as you work.

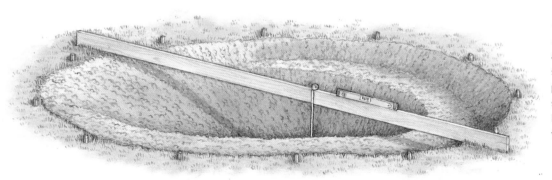

2 Use a board and level to check that the sides are level. Remove at least 6in (15cm) sod around the staked area, and use subsoil—packed down hard—to level the sides. Lay the sand, underlay, and liner, then check again to make sure the pool edges are level.

3 Carefully add the soil and gravel layers, patting them into shape. Take care not to puncture the liner. Fill slowly by allowing the hose to trickle the water in over a piece of underlay or flat stone. Allow the water in the pond to settle for a day or two before introducing any plants.

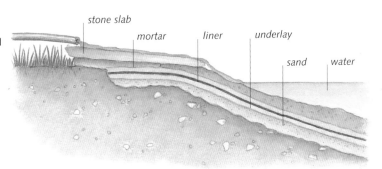

*stone slab* *mortar* *liner* *underlay* *sand* *water*

*Above* A soft mixture of plants around a pond with the early flowering *Prunus* 'Tai Haku,' the great white cherry, situated so that its foliage reflects together with the sky in the water. Nearby on the bank is the handsome royal fern (*Osmunda regalis*) with shrubs and grasses.

4 You can plant directly into the layer of soil and gravel, causing as little disturbance as possible. The water will cloud but soon clear. Check with the nursery that you are getting the correct depth of planting, and match plant vigor to the size of your pool. Then introduce floating oxygenating plants.

# Water and wetland

It was astonishing to find water striders trying out the surface of the newly made little semicircular pool in our garden almost before the water filling it had stopped running. This dash to take advantage of an additional habitat is not an isolated occurrence. There seems to be a bush telegraph that lets local wildlife know at once where a pond is being established. Initially, there may be disproportionate plant growth, but in most cases the pool will settle into a balance that requires little or no interference.

It is a good idea to establish some oxygenating aquatic plants in a new pool to provide for the water snails and microfauna and prevent the water from becoming stale and stagnant. Pondweeds (*Elodea canadensis*) and the denser, more gray-green *E. callitrichoides*, hornworts (*Ceratophyllum demersum* and *C. submersum*), as well as the beautiful feathery *Myriophyllum aquaticum* are all easily grown and look attractive. Although they will grow readily from pieces thrown into the pond, it is

better to tuck them into the silt of the pond bottom. Mosquito plant (*Azolla caroliniana*) is a pretty floating species that, like the water hyacinth (*Eichhornia crassipes*), can be simply dropped into the water.

Which aquatic plants you choose is a matter of personal preference and local climatic conditions, but always dispose of any surplus onto the compost heap and not into a nearby waterway. Alien water plants have caused serious problems through rapid and vigorous colonization. The water hyacinth, for example, has become so pernicious that it has been banned in some U.S. states, although it remains an attractive and useful pond plant in a garden environment.

Underwater plants also provide cover for secretive underwater creatures. Water snails (species of *Lymnaea*, *Planorbis*, and *Viviparus*) are more acceptable than their terrestrial counterparts, because they clean up decaying animal matter and

*Below* **A simple but striking raised brick pool and birdbath are the main features of this small scent- and color-filled terrace, with its billows of lady's mantle (*Alchemilla mollis*) and easy-going *Lilium regale* in large pots. Cut lady's mantle back after flowering and it will soon make fresh growth.**

are generally much less concerned with nibbling living plants. Water beetles, water striders, and water boatmen are among other larger invertebrates that find their way into garden ponds, along with the larvae and nymph forms of dragonflies, stone flies, and mayflies.

Frogs, toads, and newts also take full advantage of garden ponds, the species varying according to country. Green frogs (*R. clamitans*) and bullfrogs (*R. catesbina*) are the most usual garden frogs, with some *Hyla* species present in warmer states. While you can buy bullfrog tadpoles, keep in mind that they get quite large (adults can capture small birds). A friend with a water garden populated by green frogs or other smaller species will more than likely have tadpoles to spare in summertime.

If the pond has inviting shallows, birds certainly will visit to drink and bathe, and in times of drought thirsty mammals may be drawn to the water.

*Above*  A natural beach effect: This shaded, humid stone-edged pool contains delightful small water lilies (*Nymphaea*) and water hawthorn (*Aponogeton distachyos*), overhung with clumps of bergenia on one side and giving onto rocks and pebbles on the other.

*Left*  The simplest ideas are often the best: stone steps set into a bank, with a carefully controlled water flow and a natural woodland edging of snowdrops, violets, and wild arum, make a fall of great charm and naturalness.

*All green plants need sun and water to live, but in different proportions. This section of the book looks at the vast range of plants flourishing in the dryest parts of the temperate world and suggests ways of combining them for a natural effect that is also in tune with the local landscape. Even in countries where rain falls plentifully, drought is becoming common due to increased water demand. Garden use of water, although proportionally very small, is inevitably needed when resources can least cope.*

*Opposite* A dry, rocky garden superbly set among the California hills. In contrast to the tall stone pine (*Pinus pinea*), the rocky plateau has a lowish, informal planting of herbs such as rosemary, and lavender, mound-forming dry-ground shrubs, and ground-hugging species.

# Hot spots and dry places

It makes sense to be self-sufficient in water use within a garden—by using drought-resistant plants, for example. Such plants have developed different ways of dealing with their situation and climate. In the Mediterranean they have a double dormancy, closing down their growing systems in the hottest part of the year to minimize water evaporation. Some plants develop the capacity to synthesize oils that decrease evaporation and defend the plant from insect damage. Foliage may be dark, leathery, and protective, or reflective in grays and silvers, with downy or curved surfaces and stems that may be angled away from the sun's glare. Some slow-growing drought-tolerant plants thrive best in dry, barren, and infertile conditions.

Silvery-leaved shrubby plants make a worthy contribution to a dry garden in the form of artemisias (*Artemisia absinthium* or the smaller *A. stelleriana*, with its daintily lobed leaves), fragrant silvery-leaved lavenders (*Lavandula*), and lavender cotton (*Santolina chamaecyparissus*). There are softly silvery perennials, such as the tall, bushy Russian sage (*Perovskia atripcifolia*) with its strong violet-blue late-season flowers, and furry lamb's ears (*Stachys byzantina*), which makes such a good foil for bright plants such as sun-loving geraniums, and rose verbena (*Verbena canadensis*), or for the many kinds of bulbs, such as the nodding onion (*Allium cernuum*), that rise rapidly to flower in dry conditions and then lie low beneath the baking ground. The key to a naturalistic display of such plants is to build up a flow of plants that associate well. This is the type of garden in which you bask in heat, color, and scent.

*Left* Autumn joy sedum (*Sedum* 'Herbstfreude') loves hot places and stays handsome throughout the season, with its gray-green spring foliage, its colorful, flat summer flower heads, and its autumn contrasts; in winter the seeds are welcomed by birds and insects.

# Natural designs for hot, dry places

*Below* **A garden of hot midsummer color, with pink-headed** *Allium afflatunense*, **lemon-yellow** *Sisyrinchium striatum*, **and hardy geraniums as the main players. The old-fashioned chimney pot provides an informal sculptural effect.**

The beautiful bulbs, perennials, and shrubs that enjoy hot, dry conditions are tempting to any gardener, although it is not always easy to design a place for them within the garden as a whole. They tend to struggle and call for special care if planted in normally moist and fertile beds in competition with more robust plants. This group of plants prefers conditions more akin to those of their origins, although it sometimes takes a little

ingenuity to place them appropriately. Sometimes the answer is obvious: a bed with full sun for most of the day, for example.

Most gardens, however, can provide suitable conditions if you seek them: the base of a south-facing wall or the paved surface of a terrace or patio; the upper part of a bank or the cracks and fissures in a wall; a small bank of well-drained ground where more moisture-loving plants fail to

thrive; or even a rocky south-facing slope that has shallow, fast-draining soil and tends to become quite hot in the summertime.

The actual design will be influenced by the shape of the hot, dry area and its boundary walls or paths. As a general rule, the planting can be fairly sparse. While you need to make sure that all the plants are seen to their best advantage, it is not necessary—indeed, it looks rather forced— to create a tiered hierarchy as in a conventional border. In their native conditions, most of the plants of hot, dry lands are scattered over the terrain, tall ones such as sea hollies (*Eryngium*) or verbascums rising high, sprawlers such as mat-forming thymes (*Thymus serpyllum*) and candytuft (*Iberis sempervirens*) carpeting the ground in between, and medium-sized alliums and gauras dotted among them. Silver- and blue-gray-leaved shrubs such as lavender or Russian sage (*Perovskia*) can provide substance within the design.

## PLANTING PLAN FOR HOT, DRY PLACES

A hot, dry site should be planted to glimmer in a haze of heat, color, and scent. Including a selection of native plants seems to anchor the design; other plants can be added to build up bloom sequence, color, and texture.

It is important to make sure that the ground is well drained (adding grit if necessary), because many of the plants typical of this habitat will perish if they become waterlogged.

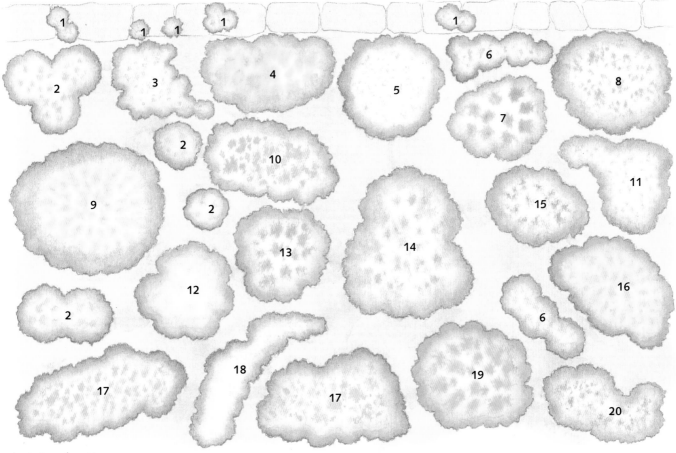

### key to planting

1 Rosy garlic *Allium roseum*
2 *Verbascum blattaria* 'Albiflorum'
3 *Allium cristophii*
4 *Euphorbia characias wulfenii*
5 *Verbascum chaixii* 'Album'
6 Vervain *Valeriana officinalis*
7 *Agapanthus campanulatus*

8 Ceanothus 'Cynthia Postan'
9 Feather grass *Stipa calamagrostis*
10 Pink *Dianthus carthusianorum*
11 Perennial flax *Linum perenne*
12 Oriental poppy *Papaver orientale* 'Cedric Morris'
13 Opium poppy *Papaver somniferum*

14 Lavender *Lavandula angustifolia*
15 *Perovskia atriplicifolia*
16 Giant feather grass *Stipa gigantea*
17 *Geranium sanguineum*
18 *Gaura lindheimeri*
19 *Kniphofia* 'Prince Igor'
20 Thyme *Thymus vulgaris*

## Garden walls

It is not as well appreciated as it should be that the flora of cliff faces in mountainous regions finds a happy counterpart in stone and brick walls in the garden. Such walls, often self-seeded, can have a stunning impact. I recall a high limestone wall aflame with fragrant wallflowers (*Erysimum cheiri*) in reds, oranges, and golds. Although in itself quite uninteresting, a city garden wall near where I live is smothered in alpines. There are aubrietas, yellow corydalis (*Corydalis lutea*), and ivy-leaved toadflax (*Cymbalaria muralis*) spilling out in bright patches, as well as small cotoneasters. All these plants are common and unexceptional in themselves, but superb growing brilliantly against the gray wall in the full sun. Recently *Erigeron karvinskianus* from Central America has joined the planting. The tiny daisy flowers of this plant (sometimes known as Mexican fleabane) open off-white and fade through pink to crimson. This

*Above* Mexican fleabane (*Erigeron karvinskianus*) is here thoroughly naturalized and at home in a warm dry-stone wall. These diminutive daisy-type plants love to grow in crevices in walls and between paving.

*Left* A dry-stone wall with common polypoly (*Polypodium vulgare*), variegated ivy, and catmint (*Nepeta* x *faassenii*) growing in it. The yellow daisies of *Doronicum excelsum* 'Harpur Crewe' and pale blue *Veronica gentianoides* grow happily in the meadow behind the wall.

spreading perennial is hardy in zones 5–7 and is just one of the many charming erigerons that are becoming popular in U.S. gardens. Most require fertile, well-drained yet evenly moist soil in summer and do not tolerate wet soil in winter—conditions provided admirably by a dry-laid stone wall, where roots can delve back into moist, cool soil, but excess water drains quickly away.

Rock gardens per se have a slightly old-fashioned feel, and artificially constructed ones that use rock trucked in from another location almost always look hopelessly unnatural in a landscape designed on natural principles. To grow a wide range of alpines, it is better to plant in a garden wall, which will take up much less space than a conventional rock garden.

To establish alpines in walls, some books tell you to scrape out the mortar and stuff in small plants or seeded potting mix, but in my view colonization is usually more successful when carried out by the plants themselves. This will be difficult in a new wall with hard pointing. In such cases, making a few scrapes to create small ledges between the bricks and the mortar enables a little organic matter to

*Above* **Gray stone steps and paving beautifully set off by sweeps of pink-red and purple** *Salvia officinalis* **'Purpurascem' and red valerian (** *Centranthus ruber* **). When the flowers die back, the salvia foliage and the ivy on the steps will create a softening effect in dark green and blue-green.**

accumulate and air- or bird-borne seeds to find a crevice in which they can germinate. Grow suitable plants in pots or in beds nearby in the hope that seeds will be blown or carried into the wall. If you are building or repairing a wall, use a soft lime-based mortar, which is more inviting to plants than the harder cements. Dry-stone walls are also attractive in themselves and can almost be considered a kind of vernacular sculpture in their own right.

*Above* **A mixture of plants for hot, dry conditions: *Geum* 'Red Wings' here has spiky, purple-tinged *Eryngium* x *oliverianum* growing through it and the yellow flowers of *Helichrysum* 'Schwefellicht' in the foreground.**

*Right* **Native to California and Mexico, Matilija poppy (*Romneya coulteri*), with its marvelously scented, late-summer blooms, thrives in this dry, sheltered environment beneath a living room window.**

## WALL BORDERS

The base of a wall is a much dryer than is usually recognized. This can be a disadvantage and accounts for the failure to thrive or even the death of many vines and shrubs that need normal water conditions but have been planted close to the wall. It can, however, provide a strip of brilliance as the base of an almost vertical mini garden. There is a wide range of bulbs, vines, and perennials that need dry conditions that will do well in this wall-hugging mini habitat. The narrowest of strip borders alongside a south- or southeast-facing wall can support an incredible range of plants, including herbs, climbing roses, wall-trained shrubs, bulbs, and annuals. Enrich the dry soil with some compost now and again, and you will be surprised at how readily the plants grow. The heat from the wall itself tends to bring flowers on earlier in spring and to prolong the season after summer has passed.

The wallside strip border can be quite varied. Climbing roses such as 'Handel' and 'Seagull' and *Clematis* 'Jackmanii' and 'Hagley Hybrid' can be interspersed by evergreens such as pyracanthas and ivy, with tulips, daffodils, and ornamental onions (*Allium*) at the base to provide seasonal distraction, along with herbs such as mints, marjoram, and parsley. Shrub roses such as 'Félicité Perpétue' and 'Pink Perpétue,' with drought-tolerant sedums and honesty, grow alongside shrubs that can sustain cutting back, such as butterfly bush (*Buddleja davidii*), forsythia, flowering quince (*Chaenomeles japonica*), and *Viburnum tinus*. Such a strip requires a certain amount of attention in the form of pruning, particularly of the vines. The clematis will also need supporting by trellis or wires stretched along the wall around which it can twine, while the roses, Japanese quince (*Chaenomeles*), and other plants with stout shoots can be tied onto fasteners secured into the wall.

*Opposite* **A corner of a walled garden, with a dry bed that catches the sun with hardy geraniums 'Johnson's Blue' and *Geranium clarkei* 'Kashmir White' growing with bearded iris and lady's mantle (*Alchemilla mollis*), as well as mounds of scented single pinks (*Dianthus*).**

*Above* **A hot bed of flowers and foliage in a rocky terraced garden. Variegated yuccas, crocosmia, diascias (*Diascia fetcaniensis*), and Mexican fleabane (*Erigeron karvinskianus*) vie stridently for attention. This is a combination of plants you could only conceive of under a blazing sun.**

## Design for dry ground

A naturally dry yard or a dry, sunlit bed within an otherwise green garden can provide the basis for dry-habitat plants. Many rivers throughout the world dry out in summer and run only in the rainy season, and the natural flora of such places is often spectacular. In many regions of Britain these are known as winterbournes, while in the southwestern United States they are the familiar arroyos. Unfortunately, there are now many places where a sinking water table has meant that dry beds have become permanent, and the flora has changed as the bed, lacking its wash of water, becomes silted with detritus and acquires a thin soil, which supports pioneer plants that in their turn give way to scrub.

A naturalistic dry bed takes plants from different stages of this development. It differs from the gravel bed that garden designers frequently

recommend as an alternative to grass, in the informality and self-sustaining character of the planting. Where possible, the dry bed would be made from locally available natural materials. In some cases this might be gravel, but only if the color and textures matched those of the garden and its local surroundings. In a rocky region, I have seen flat, low pieces of rock making a small but captivating horizontal alpine garden.

Dry-land plants love growing through flagstone paving and bricks, and letting plants grow up like this in a selected area such as a secret garden creates an alluring, romantic atmosphere.

Pathways that are not in regular mainline use can also harbor a range of plants. Rock rose (*Helianthemum*)—a widespread genus that is found in meadows and scrubland in Europe, both Americas, Asia, and Africa—looks spectacular in summer. It likes nothing better than to root in the crevices between flagstones and turn a pathway into a river of color in midsummer. To keep them shapely and ensure a good show each year, cut helianthemums back hard after they have flowered to prevent them from sprawling too much, especially when they may block a path.

Perennials such as Mexican fleabane (*Erigeron karvinskianus*), pussy-toes (*Anthennaria*), thymes (*Thymus*), and many daisies (*Bellis*) are pretty colonizers. Foxglove (*Digitalis purpurea*), verbascum (*Verbascum blattaria*), and other large biennials can find their way to less-used pathways and can be tolerated as long as they are not actually blocking the thoroughfare.

Annuals, too, find their place, in the form of common poppies (*Papaver rhoeas*), Welsh poppies (*Meconopsis cambrica*), and royal-blue larkspurs (*Consolida ajacis*), while bulbous plants such as three-cornered leek (*Allium triquetum*), Spanish bluebell (*Hyacinthoides hispanica*), and plants of the iris family such as sisyrinchiums and the dwarf iris (*Iris reticulata*) may invade gravel paths. To harbor a range of plants, the pathway needs crevices, cracks, or an open structure.

*Above* **A setting that is unmistakeably hot climate: The bold architecture of cacti—including the golden barrel cactus *Echinocactus grusoñii*—as well as palms, grasses, agaves, and plantains (*Musa*), dominates this section of a sun-baked, rocky Italian garden.**

*Left* **The flower heads of the pink-lavender star of Persia (*Allium christophii*), like colored sparklers, rise above a silver-white carpet of velvet-leaved lamb's ears, (*Stachys byzantina* 'Silver Carpet'). This nonflowering cultivar is used principally as a backdrop for showier garden flowers.**

## Irregular herb gardens

Over the last decade, geometry has dominated the style of herb gardens. Charming as formal gardens can be, nothing could be further from the way herbs grow in their native places in the shallow, baked soils of the Mediterranean. Our most valued culinary herbs look best and are at their most aromatic dotted over a landscape that looks on the face of it too infertile to support plant life. In the wild, these plants move. They utilize the mineral resources on one piece of ground and then grow outward to explore adjacent land; the piece left bare will later be recolonized by another species with different requirements. This movement occurs also in herb gardens and is why formal designs are difficult to manage, since the plants prefer not to stay neatly positioned but want to migrate. A more naturalistic plan for an herb garden keeps the soil poor, aiming for slower but more strongly flavored growth, and allows the plants to progress within

their allotted space. There usually has to be some weeding and pruning, since most garden conditions will be wetter and more fertile than the place of origin, but it is an easier form of management and, in its gentler, more relaxed way, an attractive means by which to grow herbs.

In many places in the world, herbs grow in grassland on rocky hillsides; you find species of thyme and pasqueflower in China growing in the harsh terrain around the Great Wall, while many herbs valued in the Americas are found in poor, gravelly ground or within rocky areas. Poor soil in a warm situation can be found in most gardens, and although natural planting dispenses with the conventional formal element, there still needs to be definition so that the herbs fit into their surroundings.

A sense of overall design can be made by means of paths around the herb area (which also makes the plants easy to reach for cooking purposes). If you live in a region with natural rock, the herb

*Below* **Dark-flowered French lavender (***Lavandula stoechas***), with lavender cotton (***Santolina chamaecyparissus***) and rosemary (***Rosmarinus officinalis***), interspersed with lavender (***Lavandula angustifolia***) and euphorbias in a boulder-strewn city herb garden.**

garden can flow from a close-mown lawn into a rock-strewn area, with herbs grown in and around the low rocks and boulders. Another approach is to set aside a self-contained part of the garden especially for herbs. In both cases, the composition can include physic herbs as well as culinary ones, although it is important to remember that big, burly plants such as angelica, fennel (*Foeniculum vulgare*), lovage (*Levisticum officinale*), purple coneflower (*Echinacea purpurea*), and elecampane (*Inula helenium*) can shade or overwhelm smaller low-growing herbs, especially if allowed to self-seed. One plant of these will provide you with height in the herb garden and also with more than enough material for use in the kitchen, whereas you will probably want several kinds of thyme and marjoram and many different pinks (*Dianthus*).

Our herb gardens are in fact extremely cosmopolitan. Basil (*Ocimum basilicum*) was imported to the Mediterranean from the Old World tropics before Roman times. Marjoram (*Origanum vulgare*), a European native, has naturalized readily in the northern United States. Many herbs can be transplanted and will naturalize. although it is important to remember not to spoil them by fertilizing the ground where you intend to grow them. Lavender, thyme, and marjoram all lose their piquancy in fertile soils. Although evening primroses (*Oenothera*) grow well in easier, more fertile conditions than are found in their native homelands in the United States, flowering more readily and producing plenty of seed, it has been found that the seeds no longer contain the complex essential fatty acids that are synthesized in more difficult conditions. Evening primroses prefer poor, well-drained, and even rocky soil for best growth.

## Dry banks

A dry bank looks superb with statuesque tiers of shrubs, grasses, and sturdy perennials planted to present a varied composition of foliage to create long-lasting contrast. Textures can range from airy and feathery to dense and heavy, while colors include greens, grays, copper, and pewter with the

*Above* Informality with herbs: fennel (*Foeniculum vulgare*), chives (*Allium schoenoprasum*), and golden marjoram (*Origanum vulgare* 'Aureum'), growing with cerise and silver *Lychnis coronaria* and Oriental poppies.

*Left* The big, velvety leaves of verbascum contrast with the foliage detail of small plants: the sage *Salvia officinalis* 'Tricolor' and golden marjoram (*Origanum vulgare* 'Aureum'). These are ornamental cultivars.

lime- and yellow-greens of euphorbias. This kind of planting is practical as well as ornamental, since the plants stabilize the usually thin soils of dry banks and help to prevent the erosion of steep banks.

On a larger bank, drought-resistant trees and shrubs such as junipers make a dense block of dark evergreen foliage that can be offset by the larger euphorbias such as *Euphorbia characias characias* (or *E. c. wulfenii*). On an acidic or neutral soil, brooms (*Genista* and *Cytisus*) do well, with a wide range of flower colors from mahogany red-brown to palest cream-lemon. One of the most attractive and unusual members of the broomlike family is *Adenocarpus deccorticans*, a plant that originates in Spain and does well on dry soils and banks, producing brilliant yellow flowers and sensuous, silver silken leaves. Lavender (*Lavandula*) and lavender cotton (*Santolina*) look very attractive on large banks that have a neutral to slightly

*Opposite* Plants spill over dry terraces: the wallflower 'Harpur Crewe' flowers below, while *Euphorbia characias characias* makes green-gold candelabras in front of the clipped conifers (*Chamaecyparis lawsoniana* 'Fletcheri').

alkaline soil, and have the advantage of growing quite slowly and in fairly compact cushions. *Santolina pinnata* subsp. *neapolitana*, with its greenish rather than gray foliage and pale yellow flowers, is particularly good. Scattered clumps of grasses such as the neat blue-leaved fescues (*Festuca*), handsome *Helictotrichon sempervirens*, and the tall but dainty *Stipa gigantea* provide a necessary contrast to plants with bright flowers, such as the magenta angel's fishing rod (*Dierama pulcherrimum*) or bearded irises and mulleins (*Verbascum*).

On very dry, stony, and rocky banks, sedums and saxifrages will readily naturalize, while pinks (*Dianthus*) and small ornamental onions such as *Allium sphaerocephalon* make small bright spots of crimson. Banks should not be planted too thickly or too diversely, in my view. There already exists the drama of the rising ground, and the eye should be able to travel from one plant to another enjoying the individual shape, colors, and silhouettes. There is nothing to be gained by trying to emulate the crowded, bright medley of the conventional border.

*Below left* A dry, rocky hillside overflows with plants, including *Helleborus argutifolius* in the shade, bamboo in the dappled area, and brooms (*Cytisus*), hardy geraniums, and silver-leaved shrubs on the sunlit slopes.

*Below right* A naturalized grouping, with oxeye daisies (*Leucanthemum vulgare*) taking the dominant role, carmine rose campion (*Lychnis coronaria*) the centerpiece, and tiny Johnny-jump-up (*Viola tricolor*) below, with red poppies (*Papaver rhoeas*) growing in the distance.

Meadows have a poignant impressionistic beauty that has touched the hearts and minds of poets and artists from the early Celts to the European and American painters of the nineteenth and early twentieth centuries, and it is therefore no surprise that we desire to grasp some of their glory in our gardens. The thrilling medley of grasses and flowers described by Chaucer and Guillaume de Lorris in the Romaunt of the Rose still has the power of romance for us in modern times.

*Opposite* **Purple coneflowers (*Echinacea pupurea*) flourishing in late summer on a bankside, with lilies, agapanthus, coleus (*Solenostemon scutellariodes*), and shrubs. The coneflower seed heads can be very attractive and may be left over winter. Alternatively, take a string trimmer to the dead stems.**

# Garden meadows

By incorporating a meadow area, we can vary the pace of the garden and escape the thrall of the lawn mower and the monotony of close-mown grass. There are few more attractive ways of improving a grassy area than making a wildflower meadow. It is generally thought that such meadows require considerable space, but if you choose the species carefully it is possible to have a meadow sward in a tiny area. I have a spring mini meadow consisting simply of snowdrops (*Galanthus nivalis*) and small wild daffodils (*Narcissus pseudonarcissus*), backed up with checkered lilies (*Fritillaria meleagris*) and, at the shaded edge, dogtooth violets (*Erythronium*). Only one of these—the daffodil—is truly native to my local area, while the others have naturalized in the immediate locality.

Choosing native and naturalized plants on an international basis means that you have an opportunity to design a meadow tailored precisely to your own requirements in terms of flowering time, composition, and scale, relating your choice of plant to the wildflowers that grow around you and to the range of plants that grow in similar conditions elsewhere. Most gardens in temperate regions will support a meadow tuned in this way to the local flora and conditions. Plants from various geographical meadow types, however, may climax at different times, and it is therefore preferable to use a distinct kind as a model.

*Left* After the springtime orchids, snake's-head fritillaries, and daffodils, this summer meadow settles to a simple but beautiful mixture of oxeye daisies (*Leucanthemum vulgare*) and hawkbit (*Leontodon hispidus*).

### How to make a meadow

Before you start a meadow garden, take time to learn about the plants that grow naturally in your area. The best choices will vary depending on where you live—plants that thrive in cool New England summers will not survive in the hot, dry Southwest. Wildflowers that thrive in abandoned fields and roadsides in your area are usually good choices. In most cases, you will need to remove the existing lawn in order to establish meadow plants, because vigorous rhizomatous lawn grasses will outcompete all but the most aggressive perennial plants.

One way to create a meadowlike lawn is to plant hardy spring bulbs right through the grass in the fall. The bulbs will flower and their foliage will ripen and die back by early summer, after which you can begin mowing for the season. If asked to compete with tough lawn grasses, however, most bulbs will have to be replaced every few years.

For a permanent meadow planting, plan on dispensing with vigorous creeping grasses such as Kentucky bluegrass (*Poa pratensis*) and Bermuda grass (*Cyndon dactylon*). Instead, combine bulbs and perennials with clump-forming grasses such as broomsedge (*Andropogon virginicus*), sweet vernal grass (*Anthoxanthum odoratum*), sideoats gramma grass (*Bouteloua curtipendula*), fescues (*Festuca*), and little bluestem (*Schizachyrium scoparium*). Slow-creeping grasses such as buffalo grass (*Buchloe dactyloides*) also are suitable. For a planting that looks like a lawn, stick to low-growing perennials that will survive occasional mowing. Alternatively,

## WILDFLOWER MEADOWS: A SEASONAL GUIDE

No style of planting more readily evokes the term "natural garden" than the wildflower meadow. When planted successfully it gives you a mass of color for much of the year—from the spring lawn and alpine meadows, through the wildflower lawns and grasslands of mid- to high summer, to the late-summer flowering of the prairies.

### SPRING LAWN

Hardy, small spring-flowering bulbs bloom early in the season through lawn grass, and the area can be used as a normal lawn from early summer on.

**SELECTED PLANTS** Winter aconites (*Eranthis hyemalis*), snowdrops (*Galanthus nivalis*), daffodils (*Narcissus pseudonarcissus*), crocuses (*Crocus*).

**MOWING AND CARE** After flowering, wait until foliage has died away—mow as normal from late spring. Make sure your winter lawn is well mown and neat. If the snowdrops become congested after a few years, divide them after flowering, while still green, and replant. Plant new bulbs each autumn as needed.

### ALPINE MEADOWS

Low-growing plants for spring in temperate regions.

**SELECTED PLANTS** Checkered lily (*Fritillaria meleagris*), Spanish bluebells (*Hyacinthoides hispanica*), reticulated iris (*Iris reticulata*), moss pink (*Phlox subulata*), primrose (*Primula vulgaris*).

**MOWING AND CARE** In mild winters when grass grows, mow in very early spring; otherwise leave until flowers have faded and seeded and foliage has died back, then mow regularly to about 3in (7.5cm).

you might like to consider a meadow or prairie planting with showy taller grasses and flowers. Look for a seed mixture developed especially for your particular region.

To start a meadow from seed, in spring or autumn remove the turf and till the ground twice, two weeks apart, to help control weeds. Incorporate organic matter if the soil is heavy, but do not fertilize—meadow plants don't require the rich soil conventional lawn grasses do. Or, sow seeds in a nursery bed and grow them into sturdy young plants, which can be planted out in drifts to create a natural-looking planting.

*Right* **Spring into summer with meadow plants, including Spanish bluebells (*Hyacinthoides hispanica*), columbine (*Aquilegia vulgaris*), Jacob's ladder (*Polemonium caeruleum*), and the pink flowers of *Nomocharis farreri*.**

### FLOWER-STUDDED WILDFLOWER LAWN

Medium-high plants flowering from early to midsummer. Will withstand some foot traffic after flowers have died down.

**SELECTED PLANTS** Bugleweed (*Ajuga reptans*), yarrow (*Achillea millifolium*), English daisies (*Bellis perennis*), sweet woodruff (*Galium odoratum*), field woodrush (*Luzula campestris*), hoary plantain (*Plantago media*), primrose (*Primula vulgaris*), self-heal (*Prunella vulgaris*).

**MOWING AND CARE** Mow once in early spring to about 3in (7.5cm), and mow again in summer after the plants have flowered. Do not fertilize.

### HIGH SUMMER WILDFLOWER GRASSLANDS

Taller plants for midsummer when the late grasses too are flowering.

**SELECTED PLANTS** Yarrow (*Achillea millifolium*), orange coneflowers (*Rudbeckia*), Queen Anne's lace (*Daucus carota*), sneezeweeds (*Helenium autumnale*), daylilies (*Hemerocallis flava* and *H. fulva*), goldenrods (*Solidago*), butterfly weed (*Asclepias tuberosa*).

**MOWING AND CARE** Cut down with a string trimmer in late winter or early spring. Cut back stems after flowering to keep the area neat, or leave seed heads for overwintering birds.

### TALL LATE-SUMMER PRAIRIE

Tall flowers in high, waving grasses.

**SELECTED PLANTS** Purple coneflower (*Echinacea purpurea*), globe thistle (*Echinops ritro*), Joe Pye weed (*Eupatorium purpureum*), miscanthus grass (*Miscanthus sinensis*), New England asters (*Aster novae-angliae*), prairie blazing-star (*Liatris pycnostachya*).

**MOWING AND CARE** Nurse these big, clumpy plants through the first 2–3 years with bare soils around roots until sturdy enough to compete with grass. Mow paths around groups of plants. Cut stems down in winter after seeding or in spring.

# Meadows and prairies for all seasons

You can enjoy garden meadows from early spring until late autumn. You can also plant for different heights, from low-growing snowdrops and daffodils or cropped flowering lawns, to the rangy beauty of large, clumpy plants growing along with tall grasses with paths mown through them. Make your choice according to your requirements. Mown paths through the plants will give a sense of coherence to the design within the garden as a whole. You can build up a display in a more restricted space by backing it onto a boundary hedge or alcove within the garden.

## Meadows from winter

The dominant model for the early spring meadow is that of the poetry of the *Romaunt of the Rose*, interpreted into visual form in medieval tapestries such as *La Dame à la Licorne* and the gorgeous *Book of Hours* and other illuminated manuscripts that have found their way into museums all over the world. The earliest flowers to bloom in velvet winter grass, drenched with dew or whitened by frost and kept low by grazing or mowing, are the snowdrops (*Galanthus*) and winter aconites (*Eranthus hyemalis*), closely followed by early

*Right* **Daffodils, checkered lilies (***Fritillaria meleagris***) in both red and white forms, as well as wood anemones (***Anemone nemorosa***) make a strong spring meadow combination that is easy to establish in a damp lawn. Planted in the fall, they will begin flowering the following spring.**

daffodils and primroses of various kinds. There are named varieties of snowdrop, but for a natural garden I feel you can not do better than the common, elegant *Galanthus nivalis*. Fragrant grape hyacinths (*Muscari*) and bright blue scillas (*Scilla biflora* and *S. siberica*) naturalize readily, as do crocuses. In my opinion, these small, mostly bulbous plants look their best in self-contained groupings.

The low plants that bloom earliest in the year enable those of us with quite small gardens to engage in meadow gardening, because lawns are not generally in use in this cold season. The succession of flowers may be appreciated, and after they have faded the leaves should be allowed to die back untouched so they can replenish the bulbs or corms for the next year. The meadow area should be mown before it is required as lawn for the rest of the year. This can be done with a standard lawn mower, providing the first mowing can be made with the blades somewhat higher than normal. Take the grass down in stages, allowing the plants to retire completely beneath the surface and remain dormant until the next year.

The coming of spring can be variable, but is generally heralded by daffodils. Those that are closest to the wild types are the most successful for meadow plantings, and they should be planted in drifts of one kind, except for the small hoop-petticoat daffodil (*Narcissus bulbocodium*), which looks best dotted over a bank or threaded through damp short grass so the blooms twinkle engagingly through the green carpet. It needs good drainage and does not do well in heavy soils, where the first daffodils might be 'February Gold' or some other of the small *N. cyclamineus* cultivars characterized by their narrow trumpets and thrown-back tepals. They are dainty but very hardy and able to stand up to almost any weather a cold spring can fling at them. Later, as the weather warms, the scented small-trumpet narcissus of the *N. poeticus* type fills the air with fragrance, as other spring plants such as early primroses come into flower.

Crocuses are also plants of early spring, and the species look far more natural in grass than the large-flowered Dutch hybrids. Snow crocuses (*Crocus chrysanthus*) are small and come in a range of colors, and blue-purple flowered *C. tommasinianus* is one of the most elegant species. Slightly later to appear, *Corydalis solida* naturalizes surprisingly well. Because its foliage vanishes beneath the soil very soon after the flowers have faded, the grass can be mowed almost at once. *Anemone blanda* will naturalize in lighter soils and can be grown in drifts of blue or white, pink, and blue. Checkered lily (*Fritillaria meleagris*) takes well to garden meadows, especially those that are slightly damp. It also thrives on heavier soils and will increase steadily in conditions to its liking.

*Above* **A late spring meadow, with a lovely combination of the beautifully scented poet's narcissus (*Narcissus poeticus*) and naturalized camassia (*Camassia quamash*).**

*Left* ***Chaerophyllum hirsutum* 'Roseum' is a choice pink-flowered constituent of alpine meadows that has translated to gardens, where it grows just as well in company with oxeye daisies (*Leucanthemum vulgare*) and other late spring-flowering plants. It has the same habit of growth as cow parsley.**

### Flowering lawns

The lure of a lawn often remains strong despite being labor-intensive and prone to problems, and if, for reasons of space or social use, you decide to retain it, this need not stop you from growing meadow flowers as well. Quite a wide range of plants live and sometimes flower in low grass.

*Right* Allow a lawn to grow for just a few weeks and it may well surprise you. Even common plants such as buttercups and a few bluebells can look glorious, as here with a small rocky outcrop and sinuous beds, usually associated with close-cropped lawns. It can be restored to neat lawn when the flowers and foliage die back.

*Below* Mushrooms can be a fascinating addition to a lawn. Species such as shaggy inky cap mushrooms (*Coprinus comatus*) do no damage. Watch them turn from pristine whiteness to inky deliquescence.

They are mostly plants that used to grow originally by tracks and waysides and whose seeds are often carried by passing animals or people.

Start by letting your lawn grow a bit longer than usual, and look for signs of perennials that are normally considered weeds but become welcome additions to a flowering lawn. These include buttercups (*Ranunculus*), self-heal (*Prunella*), bugleweed (*Ajuga*), and clovers (*Trifolium*). Wild strawberries (*Fragaria virginiana* and *F. vesca*) may find their way into the lawn as well, and their spring fruits are tasty for gardeners who get to them before birds and other wildlife find them. If your soil is acidic, you may find bluets (*Houstonia*). If one particular species (sometimes an unlikely candidate) begins to dominate the lawn, you may have to take control measures. Do not immediately rush into action, however, since you may find that in the next year the offending plant may have retired to reasonable proportions. Gardens are dynamic, and if you are enlisting the aid of nature it is sometimes more interesting to refrain from doing the conventional thing and watch what happens.

Much depends on the personal tastes and tolerances of the gardener. Some gardeners worry about moss invading the shady areas of their lawns, for example, while others take steps to encourage it. (Since moss thrives in acidic soil, reducing soil pH is an effective method.) Moss lawns are an elegant, low-maintenance alternative to lawn grass on a shady site, where lawns struggle to survive anyway.

When deciding what is a weed and what isn't in your garden, keep in mind that a natural garden is luxuriant in its growth but it has an essential order rather than a disregard for neglect. Rampant weeds are as untidy and out of place in a natural-style garden as in any other, and just as much of a nuisance.

*Opposite* Some cultivated tulips will continue to bloom reliably in meadow conditions, providing soil conditions are suitable. Ideally, they like a light, well-drained soil in a sunny place. A few tough varieties, such as the old-fashioned red 'Apeldoorn,' will bloom even in heavy, wetter soils.

## Prairie meadows

The crown for the most flamboyant late summer plants has to go to the flora of North America. However, although the showy prairie plants that thrilled the first settlers have been used extensively in meadow landscapes over the last century, Europeans were unenthusiastic about this style until fairly recently. Some plants were brought over to Europe from the United States in colonial times and given local names—New England aster (*Aster novae-angliae*) was adopted as Michaelmas daisy—while some names given by the American settlers were taken over, including spiderwort (*Tradescantia*) and goldenrod (*Solidago*).

True prairies, like other kinds of meadow, have 80 percent or more grass species in their composition, which means that the bold, bright colors of the late-flowering plants are muted by the green and gold matrix of stems and grass flower heads. This is not the impression that the wildflower catalogs convey. Some of their seed mixtures contain no grasses at all and often include annuals and introductions. The would-be prairie

gardener has an initial choice to make: whether to play true to the original concept and plant grasses with a roughly correct proportion of wildflowers; to aim for a meadow-prairie effect without the grasses; or whether to compromise, perhaps planting a select few of these beautiful clumping plants into an existing summer meadow to extend the season.

Making a selection of native wildflowers that have proved themselves in gardens is another matter. Some, such as asters and goldenrod, have already adopted themselves into the natural landscapes of other countries, while others such as Joe Pye weed (*Eupatorium purpurea*), coneflowers (*Echinacea*), sneezeweeds (*Helenium*), penstemons, blazing star (*Liatris*), and bergamot (*Monarda fistulosa*) have become familiar garden plants all over the temperate world. Other stunning fall-blooming perennials should not be overlooked, including boltonia (*Boltonia asteroides*), which bears clouds of tiny white daisy flowers, along with rattlesnake master (*Eryngium yuccifolium*) and sundrops, or evening primroses (*Oenothera*). These and many others are becoming more readily available away from their native continent. One of the advantages of the more robust prairie plants is that they grow vigorously and quickly and will outcompete most weeds. Gardeners who cultivate prairies or meadows will have to regularly weed out tree seedlings, however.

A few late-season European plants call for a place: Globe thistles (*Echinops*) are robust enough to survive among grasses as well as in groupings without grass competition. Scabious (*Knautia* and *Scabiosa*) are attractive late-season meadow plants with blue-lilac flowers. Knapweeds (*Centaurea*) in crimson-purples are a widespread genus, similar in appearance to thistles and very attractive to butterflies and other insects.

*Left* **Wildflower seed mixture of annuals growing to splendid effect in a small garden. Mainly California and Shirley poppies (*Eschscholszia californica* and *Papaver rhoeas*), this blend may self-seed, but the soil will need cultivating each autumn.**

*Left* The large-flowered aster hybrids will not actually self-seed like the species, but they will persist for years in the right conditions, a pleasure both to people and to butterflies.

## PLANTING PLAN FOR A PRAIRIE MEADOW

A prairie border can be concentrated into a smaller area than the more open grassy prairie meadow, and it is more colorful and densely planted. Much of the planting is taken from the beautiful late-flowering species of North America, but in the prairie border they are augmented by other larger late-season flowering plants and grasses that make good clumps or drifts. The choice will depend on personal taste as well as the amount of space that can be allocated to the project and the use that will be made of the area being planted.

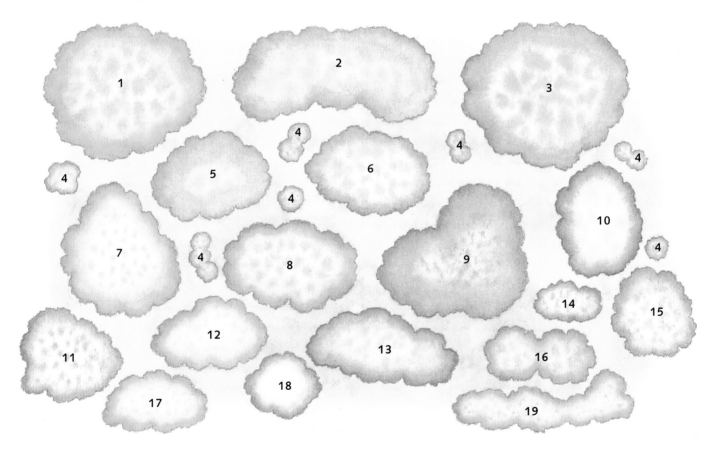

### key to planting

1 Joe Pye weed *Eupatorium purpureum*
2 Grass *Miscanthus sinensis* 'Malepartus'
3 Queen of the prairies *Filipendula rubra*
4 *Verbena bonariensis*
5 Indian grass *Sorghastrum nutans*
6 *Sanguisorba obtusa*
7 *Echinacea purpurea* 'White Lustre'

8 Purple coneflower *Echinacea purpurea*
9 Switch grass *Panicum virgatum*
10 Meadowsweet *Filipendula ulmaria*
11 Globe thistle *Echinops ritro* 'Veitch's Blue'
12 *Astrantia major*
13 Grass *Pennisetum orientale*
14 *Scabiosa caucasica*

15 Knapweed *Centaurea nigra*
16 New England aster *Aster novae-angliae*
17 Musk mallow *Malva moschata*
18 *Gaura lindheimeri*
19 Meadow cranesbill *Geranium pratense*

### Prairie borders

Prairie borders are groupings of prairie plants without the grass matrix, and are therefore more colorful and densely planted than you would ever find in the wild state. In effect, they constitute a bold late-season border that is rather less labor-intensive than the traditional border. A prairie border can be attractively augmented with other late-season selections, and grasses are planted as stars in their own right. There are some handsome authentic prairie grasses that look lovely with asters or goldenrod. One of the most beautiful is switch grass (*Panicum virgatum*), with its diffuse arcs of tiny beadlike flowers. It thrives even in poorer soils so long as it has full sun. Allow plenty of room also for the graceful, fine-textured Indian grass (*Sorghastrum nutans*), which also likes full sun and prefers a reasonably fertile soil, producing late, elegantly falling flower panicles.

In a more eclectic grouping, *Miscanthus*, with its arching silky panicles, is among the most beautiful and reliable of grasses. It needs full sun and usually does better in slightly moist conditions, although it will not tolerate being waterlogged in winter. Sedges, too, can play a part, smaller ones at the edge of the border, or taller ones, such as the easy-going pendulous sedge (*Carex pendula*), with its pendent green-brown flower heads like heavy late-summer catkins, farther into the border.

A prairie border can be planted to have the stepped effect of a conventional border or be given more natural-looking mix-and-match groupings with different heights and colors. The danger is to try to pack in too many plants and lose the sense of individual form. If you pick from different parts of the world, you also need to keep an aesthetic sense of what will combine gracefully with other plants or there will be a jarring of color and shapes. Overall, the prairie meadow is a generous, open-ended kind of gardening, where personal taste and gradually gained experience of what kinds of plant take more readily to your garden conditions make it a most exciting and experimental style.

Bold perennial plants that grow in eye-catching clumps interact with the dramatic grasses within the prairie border. Some of the rich-colored prairie plants set the tone: the red-purple *Echinacea*

*Left*  **A fanfare of summer colors, with wild, naturalized, and cultivated flowers in managed abandon: lupine, pot marigolds, red poppies, mullein, sunflowers, *Verbena bonariensis*, tiger lily, and hibiscus all vie for attention from passersby.**

*purpurea* or cultivars such as *E. p.* 'Robert Bloom,' which has a touch more crimson. Joe Pye weed (*Eupatorium purpureum*) and the stiff purple, candelabra flower heads of *Verbena hastata* add depth and richness of color to the border. Foxgloves, for midsummer, and sea hollies (*Eryngium* or *Centaurea*, for example), later in the season, can be interspersed between the larger plants. The effect is lifted with pale-toned plants such as *Lysimachia clethroides* with its tall spires, or clouds of white-flowered *Crambe cordifolia* in midsummer, while the dense, tight, creamy wands of Culver's root (*Veronicastrum virginicum*) and *Verbascum chaixii* flower from late-summer into autumn. Purple-leaved smoke tree (*Cotinus*) or evergreens such as conifers, holly, or boxwood can be used to create an attractive backdrop.

*Left* A damp meadow in Colorado with native species on a sunny June day, displaying yellow daisylike flowers known as mule's ears, and scarlet *Gillia*. Both these plants like a moist soil as well as full sun.

*Below* Grasses are perhaps at their most dramatic on their own. Here *Stipa*, *Miscanthus*, and bamboo create an extravagant effect in a woodland clearing.

# USING A
# NATURAL GARDEN

A garden with natural style should be an inviting place that those who use it can enjoy it and where there is always something of interest. It is a place to grow herbs or pick home-grown fruit through the seasons, where children play and cats and dogs can chase or doze peacefully—but where adults also can relax and be tranquil under a green canopy of trees or beside a pool. You can take work outdoors, give yourself a quiet break, entertain a large party. You can use your garden to extend an interest in sculpture, design, plant life, or natural history at your own pace.

*Opposite Left* An informal kitchen garden in late summer, with beehives and plants that include sunflowers, broccoli, onions, and herbs. The flowering herbs and hyssop are good bee plants, while the beans in flower also have their pollinators close by.

Gardening in a natural way used to be associated with frugality and a rather rough and basic effect. The last decade or so has seen a complete change in attitude, because people have come to see that a philosophy that recognizes the importance of conserving resources and working with natural forces is not only practical but also stylish. Even compost bins have been given a new look and incorporated into garden plans by well-respected garden designers.

*Opposite* Where an artifact such as a sundial draws the eye, the surrounding planting seems to compose itself around it. Hardy geraniums and astrantia set the tone for this early-summer scene, with the small, bright carmine European gladiolus making splashes of rich color.

# Decorative elements

It cannot be said too strongly that a garden that adopts a natural style is not a wild and disorderly garden. In fact, a garden that is overgrown and out of control contains a smaller number of habitats, attracts less wildlife, and sustains fewer plant species, because the burly ones overwhelm the less robust ones and create a dominant habitat. The art of the natural garden is to identify and develop each of the natural habitats and to maintain them at their optimum. This way it will support and invite a greater range of plants and animals.

The modern style that developed from the passion for wildflower gardening in the United States and Europe (especially The Netherlands), and the recognition of the value of indigenous flora in Australia and New Zealand, has adopted a wider range of plants, although it uses them in new ways, too. A sense of design is realized in a naturalistic style that includes ornamentation and works of art. The process continues as gardeners discover new plants that are prepared to naturalize (helped in some cases by changing climatic conditions). There is enormous scope for ideas that meet the needs of environmentally conscious gardeners with smaller gardens—ideas that blend nature and artifice.

Paths, internal and external boundaries, lighting, and social areas, and their integration one with another, all play an important role within a informally relaxed but handsome garden design, which should seem perfectly appropriate to its setting, full of life, and promise.

*Left* Found items, such as logs and driftwood, make good decoration within a natural-style garden. Here, a certain amount of art has contrived a rare European alligator that slithers and slides from the undergrowth.

# Decorative projects

The old art of working with living trees has been rediscovered, and gardens are once again ornamented with skillfully made arbors and by trained fruit trees and bushes, including innovative shapes such as single-tiered espaliered apple trees, which can act as an edging to a mixed bed. Espaliers are both a controlled way of introducing additional varieties of fruit into a smaller garden as well as a beautiful and productive living trellis.

Arbors provide shelter and seating in a garden, and they can also reflect a dominant mood. You introduce a sense of solidity and permanence with the velvety dark foliage of yew, a cheerful brightness with hawthorn, and almost-instant shelter with fast-growing species such as willow.

In researching this book, I was intrigued that arbors receive no mention in several of the most compendious and comprehensive gardening dictionaries and companions. In the illustrated books, modern arbors consisted of heavy metal

structures, beams lightly dusted with wisterias, or, in one case, a very solid, wooden, arched affair with a ridiculous conglomeration of roses perched on top like a wedding hat. There were examples of other structures in willow and hazel, twined more or less successfully with vines. In other words, we seem temporarily to have lost sight of the original conception of the arbor, which was primarily a curious interweaving of living plants.

The medieval period was full of such arbors, some of them taking their inspiration from the gardening writings of Pietro Crescenzi from early in the fourteenth century, in which he described how to "plant fruit-bearing trees which can be easily interlaced, such as cherries and apple trees; or else olives or poplars which will grow quickly." Sometimes these living arbors were themselves interplanted with scented vines; in Shakespeare's *Much Ado About Nothing*, Beatrice is to go to the "pleached bower/Where honeysuckles ripened by

*Below* **The skills that create beautiful and functional willow baskets can be turned to art in willow sculptures. These woven willow geese grazing a garden lawn are full of life. The hurdle fence in the background is functional as well as attractive.**

# HOW TO MAKE AN ARBOR

Hawthorn trees can make a densely textured arbor that will be private and fairly windproof. Willow will produce quicker, more latticed results but will require more trimming. An even more rapid finish can be achieved by making a trellis framework and covering it with ivy. However, the extra time and effort involved in using hawthorn is definitely worthwhile, since it will remain crisp, need little maintenance, and last for many years.

1 Plant twelve hawthorn (*Crataegus monogyna*) barerooted whips (small trees) in autumn, three for each side, six along the back, about 16in (40cm) apart. Stake with 6ft (2m) bamboo poles. Treat as for a hedge, trimming at intervals until they grow to the required height, and trim.

2 During winter, secure a bamboo scaffold along the top of the arbor and let the leading shoots grow up. After autumn leaf fall, bend the pliable shoots over, weave them together, and tie them in.

3 During the next season, let the leaders grow (upward or at an angle) until all meet across the top of the arbor when brought to the horizontal. Tie them in and trim. Continue to trim and clip until the arbor is to your satisfaction. Thereafter, trim twice a year.

*Above* You do not need a degree in willow sculpture to enjoy making garden structures. Here, willow branches, taken from pollard prunings, have been used to made a pleasant leafy arbor. All you need do is set the willow branches into the ground—and wait.

the sun/Forbid the sun to enter." These would create an inviting shade in hot climates, where one needed respite from a persecuting sun, but in cooler climates arbors might be south-facing, presenting a warm place to sit and rest in pleasant dappled shade.

Willow arbors grow very quickly from stems set into the ground and, as Crescenzi says, their pliable shoots can be easily woven or bound together. They do not, however, stop growing when the arbor has been fashioned, and people with willow arbors must be prepared to continue weaving and pruning them regularly. Hawthorn is a traditional choice of tree material for arbors (see p. 99), and once established makes a dense texture of twigs,

small leaves, and flowers. In Britain, arbors of this kind have been created at Hatfield Palace in Hertfordshire and need only light trimming a few times each year.

To achieve an arbor of this sort, you plant as for a hedge but in the shape of an open oblong—the long side stretching far enough to accommodate the bench that will eventually be placed within, with slightly curving wings on each side of it. Be patient while the plants create a root system capable of sustaining the upward growth and, as the plants rise, trim them to shape. In the final stages you can leave the top open or bring them over in a shell-like curve, depending on your taste and the amount of sun and light you desire.

*Below* **Fairly formal garden ornaments, such as statues and urns, have an extra charm when placed within a slightly informal setting. Here, the longer grass and billowing roses create a perfect descant to the classical urn on its plinth.**

*Above* **Attention to detail is well worthwhile. A teepee support need not be starkly utilitarian but a pleasure in itself. Such a structure can be bought or made from trimmed branches, lightly woven together and secured with pliable young hazel or willow twigs, or with raffia.**

*Opposite* **Roses are not usually reckoned to have much decorative value in wintertime, but their long, pliable whippy shoots make them ideal for arches. A scented climber, such as 'Dortmund,' would be excellent.**

# Natural ornaments and accessories

On first consideration, one might imagine that sculpture and garden artifacts, such as sundials, birdbaths, or even garden furniture would be out of place in a natural style of garden. In practice, art in many forms works exceptionally well. This means not simply the rounded, weathered-look natural shapes of a Henry Moore or Barbara Hepworth sculpture but also more formal works. Even if the surrounding vegetation has become a little overgrown, the presence of an artifact at a strategic point gives an impression of convergence, so it appears to be an intentional composition. Sometimes a rock in a striking shape will make

a considerable impact on its own as a natural sculpture. In my region of southeast England, rock is scarce and people have for centuries cherished the few large pieces: sandstone sarsens brought in during the Ice Age, and a kind of prehistoric cemented rock, known as pudding stone, that consists of pebbles trapped together in a silicate matrix. They may be found in fairly large pieces that in the past were incorporated into sacred shrines and old church walls but are also given pride of place in gardens. Native fieldstone makes lovely walls for a natural garden, whether rough-cut and mortared or hand-piled. There are a few sculptors

*Below* **Stone seals flecked with lichens on a sea of garden bluebells (***Hyacinthoides***), with the biogeneric hybrid x *Fatshedera lizei*. It is a good bet that the more artlessly casual the effect, the more thought and care will have gone into the placing of a sculpture.**

who have used native rock, including granite and sandstone, to carve pieces of considerable flair. The ideal might be to find exactly the right piece of sculpture at an exhibition or even to commission one. There are outdoor galleries, devoted entirely to artworks for the garden, that have occasional garden works for sale, and some of the big auction houses (Sotheby's, for example) have dedicated sales grounds. The works of art include everything imaginable, from small items of sculpture to huge statues or wellheads, as well as benches, stone and iron balustrades, and topiary.

It is, however, possible to find nice things, even on a very limited budget. If you choose carefully, you can discover interesting and well-made artefacts at garden centers and stores. In a local garden warehouse, I found a small stone frog for my own pond, superior to many at several times the price. It is also well worth looking in at architectural and builders' salvage yards. It is astonishing what ingenuity good materials can inspire in people: a small fountain head pieced together from different pieces of stone; a checker-board herb garden out of a job lot of square blocks of limestone; fountains made of huge driftwood

*Above* This eye-catching statue plays a key role in nut plantation, with the plants beneath chosen for spring flowering and illuminating lime-green coloration: *Smyrnium perfoliatum, Euphorbia amygdaloides robbiae,* Bowles' golden grass (*Milium effusum* 'Aureum'), wood anemones, sweet woodruff (*Galium odoratum*), and *Trilium sessile.*

*Left* Ceramic deva houses, situated so that they attract nearby divine spirits within the gently toned flowers of this California herb garden, with its lemon-yellow mullein spires and salvia flowers of china blue.

# Entertaining and lighting

There can be few pleasures more complete than entertaining friends in a garden setting. Food seems more delicious, conversation more interesting—and the world an altogether better place out of doors, amid the flowers and foliage.

While I enjoy picnics as much as anybody, I feel that these are for traveling abroad, or days out. At home, I like to eat at a table. There is a lot of well-made, well-designed garden furniture for sale, but while there is no shortage of choice, you need to make sure it is the right size and style for your garden. You do not, for example, want to have to wrestle with heavy furniture each time a meal outdoors takes your fancy, nor is it pleasant to

watch expensive purchases deteriorating before your eyes because they are exposed to the weather. Some garden furniture is designed to be left outdoors—certain hardwoods look better after a few years than they did when new, because the weathering process modifies the color. It would, however, be a pity if gardens in the Western world were promoting natural style at the expense of tropical forests, so it is important to check that such furniture was made from lumber grown in properly managed forests.

Cast-iron and aluminum furniture will last many years as long as you can make sure the paint is in reasonably good condition and chips are quickly

*Below* **A flowery grove of columbines, meadow grass, Welsh poppies, and garden angelica in a wooded alcove with a presiding bust, where you could equally well relax with a drink, take a pile of work, or simply enjoy the sights and sounds of the garden.**

covered. Powder coating has meant that the surfaces are very well protected, so usually it is only light touching up that is necessary.

If the design is good, garden furniture can itself be a pleasure to look at, a kind of sculpture you can use. It also has to be comfortable, so try it as thoroughly as possible before you buy. I like to have matching chairs, some of which can be placed independently in other parts of the garden.

Sitting under a tree, so that the table is at least partly shaded, is usually a good bet. Where you put the table should also be determined by the quality of the view over the garden, and by how far you have to bring tableware and food. The golden rule for outdoor eating is to keep it simple.

Cooking outdoors is another matter, but made easier by the advent of very good portable barbecues. The simplest of these are Vietnamese cast-iron pots with a gridiron over the top to cook on. For those who make a habit of cooking outdoors, there are some excellent designs for permanent outdoor cooking fixtures in brick, with a chimney to draw off the smoke, and places for the ash, a compartment where you store wood, and other extras. If it is to be permanent, it is worth taking trouble with both the design and execution.

Hammocks can be hung from trees, walls, or free-standing posts. The South American type, made of a fine lattice of fine string, must be one of the most therapeutic products ever conceived. You lie laterally in them, and there is room to accommodate one or two people. The gentle swinging to and fro is deliciously soothing, and they are comfortable enough to sleep in overnight. Hammocks look more attractive than deck chairs or sun loungers and take up less room when stored. It is a good plan to make the fittings for them permanent. These need not be obtrusive: a rope tied to a metal hook or a coach bolt driven securely into a stout wall.

If you don't have a convenient tree to provide shade or wish to provide a shady spot on a patio, consider a large umbrella or parasol. Canvas kinds come in a variety of beautiful shapes and last for

years if stored carefully during the winter. Less expensive but just as attractive, the Asian waxed parasols are elegant and effective. They tear quite easily but last well if you are careful of them.

## Giving parties

It is pleasant to allow parties to spill out from the house or sunroom into the garden, especially if you have a patio where people can linger and talk. Some people go to elaborate lengths to wire up their gardens so as to play music in every part. Apart from the possible nuisance to neighbors, this seems unnecessarily intrusive. For my taste, the quiet of the garden should beckon from the brighter, noisier reaches of the house.

A party that extends into the night demands the safe lighting of paths and steps, and romantic illuminations elsewhere, which keeps other areas of the garden dreamily leafy and mysterious.

## Lighting

Lighting is also important for people whose working life keeps them away for most of the day and for whom garden illumination extends the possibility of enjoying the garden into late evenings in summer and autumn. Lighting is essential in terms of safety and security, too. Nothing keeps

*Above* **A Canadian concert** *fête champêtre* **(outdoor party) near Quebec. Created by the sculptor Charles Smith, this jazz quartet makes an amusing contribution to a garden where a short growing season surely makes its owners appreciate the value of the days they are able to spend out of doors.**

*Right* A typical pathside light. Such lights often come in sets of four or six, with a low-voltage transformer. There is usually the possibility of adding extra lights if you have a big garden. Lighting such as this is easy to install, cheap to run and repair, and represents very good value.

*Below* A charming and well-made brass Indian lantern. This type of lantern can be hung individually in trees or on hooks, and is lit by a brass candle that holds liquid fuel and burns with a steady flame. Alternatively, these lamps can be electrically powered and installed in sets.

would-be burglars out so usefully as lights, and they are essential in illuminating the way down paths at nighttime. Lights also give you a garden view even if you do not actually venture outdoors.

There is more to lighting the garden than utilitarianism, however. Moonlight brings a different kind of texture and surface reality to plants. Light from the moon may be strong enough to cast shadows and dapple the ground, but it is of a magical quality, entirely transforming the known garden. The moon is only bright enough to create her effects occasionally each month, but I think that subtle illumination of the garden can and should aspire to the same quality of light.

The low-level lights that are readily available at gardening stores are both effective for illuminating paths and softly discreet if hidden within or behind perennial plants so that the lights themselves are partially concealed and their beam diffused. For party use, there are delightful containers that consist of glass saucers that each hold a small candle or night light, covered by a cut-glass shade that both keeps off the worst of the wind and gives a sparkle to the gentle and flickering light.

Various kinds of flares and beacons are available for garden use, some of which have fuel containing an insect repellent. You can find ingenuous Indian lanterns fitted with a brass candle, which you fill with a special lamp oil that is odorless and smokeless (get it from a lamp or marine store). For an unsophisticated impromptu effect, collect attractive multifaceted pickle and jam jars and place a candle or night light inside.

Foliage lit from beneath looks mysterious, and the pattern of twigs in winter and the subtleties of the branching of trees are shown off to their best by soft simple lights. Personally, I find floodlights overdramatic, bleaching out the subtleties of nature rather than revealing them. Smaller white lights are a different matter; during the twelve days of Christmas, I weave a skein of white outdoor Christmas-tree lights into the branches of the medlar tree—which creates the most beautiful tracery, especially when there is a hoarfrost.

# WAYS OF LIGHTING THE GARDEN

Lighting extends your enjoyment of the garden, whether you are sitting outdoors in summer or looking out on winter tracery. Light can come from above or below, in focused spots, lanterns, low-voltage or brilliant security. It is best to experiment before you install a system and always make sure you follow safety procedures fully.

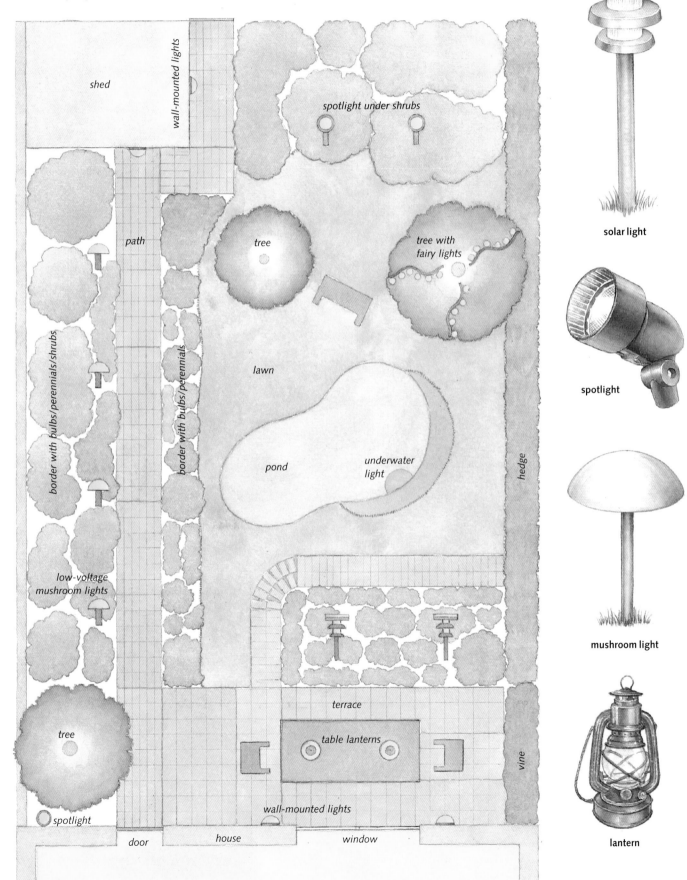

shed

wall-mounted lights

spotlight under shrubs

path

tree

tree with fairy lights

border with bulbs/perennials/shrubs

border with bulbs/perennials

lawn

pond

underwater light

hedge

low-voltage mushroom lights

tree

spotlight

terrace

table lanterns

vine

wall-mounted lights

door

house

window

solar light

spotlight

mushroom light

lantern

# Fruits, herbs, and salad greens

Food fresh from the garden is incomparably better than you can find elsewhere—not only can you choose the varieties whose flavor you like best, but the food is also guaranteed to be absolutely fresh and pesticide free. It is very much easier, too, to walk a few steps into the garden than to drive to the nearest supermarket to find vegetables that are already beginning to age. Quite apart from this, there is the satisfaction of growing for the table as well as the surprise of finding out how easy it is.

Despite the fact that my family seems always to be rushed for time, we always grow some salad greens and vegetables—the easy ones that will produce even if we have to neglect them a little. A strong consideration for me has always been that I knew our vegetables were pesticide free, so I could encourage the children to eat them whenever they felt like it. As a result, they enjoy most kinds of greens and can make a pretty delicious herb and salad sandwich if they are stuck for a snack.

With salads, fruit, and vegetables, as with nonedible plants, you match the plants you grow to soil and climate. At the very least, you can add some herbs to the sunny places and line the edge of a border with decorative lettuce plants. 'Salad

Bowl' (in red or green) is one of the most ornamental of lettuces—it tastes good and may be picked a few leaves at a time from each plant, so as not to leave gaps at harvest. Among other easily grown lettuces, I like the Batavia types (sometimes these have a touch of red to them), and both old and new kinds of romaine. Lettuces are very beautiful, especially when the young leaves start to mature and the sun shines through them.

I like to grow lettuces together in groups in one of my deep beds. These are particularly good in heavy, cold soils and are designed to be just wide enough for the gardener to be able to reach to the middle from either side. My beds are 11ft (3.5m) long and 5ft (1.5m) wide, although these proportions may be varied to suit taste and the size of the garden. I also take advantage of the fact that the soil is turned as I sow and harvest, and add a few annuals such as poppies, California poppies (*Eschscholzia*), cornflowers, and marigolds among the crops. I often grow purely ornamental plants in the part of the deep bed that is close to the main path, and I have fruit bushes in some of them, divided from the main lawn by espaliered apple trees—a design that works well and looks good.

It is surprising how much you can grow in one or two deep beds with a reasonably fertile soil, and how decorative they can look. Bunching onions grown from sets planted in early spring are the easiest and tastiest way to produce your own onions. They clump up in the summer in groups of reds and browns, depending on the varieties, that can range from quite sweet to sharp. There are few kinds of foliage more ornamental than that of carrots, and a row or two is essential, if the soil is reasonably friable. If the soil is cold and heavy and you prepare it well, choose round rather than long

*Below* **Red-stemmed Swiss chard is easy to grow and tastes delicious sliced thin in salads or lightly steamed with butter. White-stemmed chard is also available, and 'Joseph's Coat' is a cultivar with pink-, yellow-, red-, and white-stemmed plants. It is grown here with small but brilliant scarlet geraniums (*Pelargonium*).**

*Opposite* **A glamorous kitchen garden, with vegetables and flowers neatly intermingled, the golden African marigolds blazing between the greens of the cabbage, tomato, and artichoke foliage. Cosmos, dahlias, cleomes, cannas, and nicotiana provide cut flowers for the house.**

*Right* Ripening medlar fruits. A medlar makes a small and beautiful tree, hardy and easy to grow in a restricted space. It has a lovely, slighty weeping form, thick foliage, roselike flowers, and strange fruits that can either be eaten ripe with port after a few frosts have softened them or be made into a preserve.

*Below* A kitchen garden, integrated into the wider framework of the landscape, and falling to a lake. It is separated off by a lowish hedge that allows the blossoms of the apple trees to be seen from afar.

mainland, gardeners can also enjoy cherries, but in Britain they are best avoided since the birds seem to be particularly avid for this fruit.

In your own garden, fruits not readily available commercially can be grown, including quinces and medlars, along with black raspberries and pawpaws (*Asimina triloba*). Since some fruits, such as pears, have only a short period of perfect flavor and ripeness, growing your own also lets you enjoy them at their peak. Most fruits are ornamental as well as edible, and grapes, kiwifruit, and (in warmer climates) passion fruit make a useful as well as beautiful drapery for arches or trellis.

Research into ways of growing fruit has resulted in rootstocks that have greatly increased possibilities for better cropping. If you buy a named variety on a recognized rootstock from a reputable nursery, you can have fruit within a year or so and be fairly confident of the flavor and the ultimate size of your tree. With the revival of interest in fruit, you can now buy ready-trained fruit trees, skillfully shaped by an expert horticulturist. Alternatively, it is possible to train your own tree to the shape you desire: a short trunk with a goblet shape, for example, that could line a kitchen garden area; a living trellis of espalier; or a fan planted against the wall. Some of the shapes are a little extreme for a natural style and rather difficult to maintain, but an espalier is simple to do and the results are fruitful as well as decorative.

For those who prefer a naturally shaped tree, there is still a wide choice. Nearly all fruit trees are grafted, so you can have a dwarf tree to fit a small space, a tree that branches out at about shoulder height (known as half-standard), a large spreading tree (standard), or gradations in between. Quince with its pink blossom and medlar with its white roselike flowers are naturally small trees. There is also variation in size and vigor between cultivars.

*Opposite* A kitchen garden happily integrated within the leisure garden: herbs and vegetables grow alongside flowers and shrubs, while the flowering fruit trees have bulbs planted around their bases in a wide lawn.

A garden without movement and sound is inconceivable. The individual voices of birds and the characteristic flight patterns of insects can become as familiar as the personal characteristics of close family and friends. When you are in the garden, you learn to sense things on the edges of your consciousness, such as the flutter of finches. A fleeting glimpse of deer, the sharp tang of fox or tomcat, or encounters with lizards and newts—these too are all part of the garden experience.

*Opposite* Very beautiful butterflies of the colorful family *Nymphalidae*: the small tortoiseshell (*Aglais urticae*) and the peacock (*Inachis io*) sipping nectar from *Inula hookeri*. Both species of butterfly lay their eggs on nettles, the tortoiseshell preferring young tender plants, the peacock larger and more vigorous ones.

# Wildlife in the garden

You do not have to live in a wilderness to appreciate wildlife—wild creatures abound even in the center of cities. You can find them in the air or the fabric of buildings, in tree trunks, among the foliage of vines and bushes, even underfoot in the soil. Although any garden will attract some wildlife, you can purposely make it more welcoming. The more varied habitats you have and the wider the range of plants you present to the animal world, the better chance you have of attracting a diversity of wildlife. In addition, the presence of many different species in a complex mixed economy means that you are more likely to have a predator population to match those regarded as pests.

Your invitation to the natural world will almost always be answered. Provide some water in the garden or set up a bird feeder, and the response will be immediate. Build a nature-friendly wall packed with plants, create a permanent meadow or prairie planting, plant berry bushes such as viburnums for birds, or leave perennials standing over winter so visitors can enjoy their seeds. Some animals will take up residency in the garden, while others—such as migratory birds—will come as seasonal or occasional visitors.

The more your awareness grows of the complex web of life forms supported within even a quite conventional garden, the more understanding you develop. This in turn leads to a more sympathetic way of managing a garden.

*Left* This dragonfly (*Aeshna cyanea*) is remarkably unafraid of people and does not dart away like many other species of dragonfly. It lays its eggs on floating vegetation.

# Wildlife attracted to gardens

The eighteenth century saw an extraordinary renaissance in science, rational thought, and the understanding of natural history. Although people explored far and wide, sending back observations and opinions, another quieter achievement in the study of natural history was just as important and far-reaching. The naturalist parson Gilbert White (1720–93) saw that ranging abroad was not the only means of education but that careful research in one place could yield new and important knowledge, too. His own quiet but incredibly thorough inspections in his garden and its immediate environs brought several new insights to natural science and set a model that is still valid.

Garden naturalists can make their contributions. One contemporary British gardener, Dr. Jennifer Owen, watched the plants and animals in her garden over a period of fifteen years and found, when she came to summarize her findings, that a quite extraordinary number of birds, plants, spiders, and invertebrates lived alongside her. Even more startling was the fact that this ecological study was carried out, not in a rural idyll, but in a medium-sized garden in the suburb of an industrial city in the English Midlands—with a lawn, flower beds, alpine garden, neat paths, and mixed plantings of flowers, vegetables, and salad greens.

Dr. Owen's plot is a long rectangle of about 886 sq yd (741 sq m), of which slightly over a third is taken up by the house, carport, and driveway. Yet in this small compass there are several hundred kinds of plants, twenty-one kinds of butterflies, sixty-eight species of moths, and representatives of many other animal groups, such as sow bugs, bees,

*Below* A vista of mounded *Sedum spectabile*, a perennial species that not only people but also birds and insects find attractive. Clipped boxwood grows in the foreground, with yellow *Anthemis* 'E.C. Buxton' flourishing behind it.

ants, spiders, and birds. I was pleased to notice four different kinds of hover fly in my more southerly garden, but this is nothing beside Dr. Owen's keen, discerning observations. She identified hundreds of individuals and a total of ninety-one species in her garden in Leicestershire. There is a similar number of plants and creatures in almost all gardens—it is simply a matter of seeing them and of developing the food plants and places that sustain them.

Other records have shown a remarkable diversity of wildlife in urban gardens. It is now well understood that large cities such as New York have their own microclimates. Under conditions that may be a degree warmer than the surrounding countryside, wild flora and fauna thrive, and gardeners can confidently grow warmer-climate species that their rural counterparts would not dare attempt, thus providing an extra band of plants for wildlife to colonize. Mammals are also visitors to some gardens. Foxes and badgers come to European gardens and raccoons to North American ones. It is not at all unusual for hummingbirds to feed on nectar-rich shrubs and trees in city gardens

*Above* A pleasant scene in a New York community garden, with an ideal plant mixture where flowers, fruits, salad greens, and vegetables nudge along side by side. Community gardens (official and unofficial), especially those within large towns, have beneficial effects for both their human and animal residents.

*Left* A common and widespread New World species, the robin (*Turdus migratorius*) is a frequently seen visitor to urban gardens. Besides berries, it eats worms and insects, nesting in shrubs and trees, on sheltered windowsills, and under the eaves of houses.

in California, and other birds such as mockingbirds, orioles, wrens, blue jays, chickadees, and cardinals frequent gardens in many states.

It used to be said that native species of plants were always superior to introductions and exotics in terms of the abundance of wildlife they can support. Subsequent research has shown a more complex pattern, with many garden introductions and naturalized plants scoring very highly for wildlife benefit. Many garden flowers are extremely rich in nectar, and in many gardens nonnatives provide early and late blooms that are vital to end-of-season insects.

Native plants are especially important where they form part of a complex cycle of nutrition and breeding, such as that of the blue butterflies (*Lycaenidae*). Studies found that their cycle involves fine-grazed grass growing in the right site, special food plants, and ants that look after the butterfly chrysalis and larva.

The lives of insects are a small marvel of unbelievable complexity and to try to replicate precise conditions to entice a rarity into the garden would be very difficult. Starting from the opposite position and growing plants that are known to attract butterflies, and especially the favorites of those species you have actually seen in the garden,

*Opposite* **Three late-season garden bumblebees, of the commonest garden species (*Bombus hortorum*), explore the florets of the beautiful eryngium known as giant sea holly (*Eryngium giganteum*). This late-flowering eryngium is a welcome supply of late nectar for insects.**

## FLOWERS THAT ATTRACT BIRDS, AND BUTTERFLIES, BEES, HOVER FLIES, AND OTHER INSECTS

**asters** *Aster novae-anglia, A. novi-belgii, etc.*
   butterflies, moths, and other late-feeding insects; birds eat seeds

**aubretias** *Aubretia*
   attract butterflies that have hibernated as adults, and other flying insects

**buddleja** *Buddleja davidii*
   butterflies, moths, hummingbirds, hawk moths, and other insects

**hawthorns** *Crategus*
   provide shelter and berries for birds; nectar, pollen, and foliage for moths and butterflies

**purple coneflowers** *Echinacea*
   flowers attract bees and butterflies; birds eat seeds

**ivies** *Hedera helix*
   late flowers for butterflies, bees, moths; berries for birds; shelter

**hops** *Humulus*
   food for butterfly larvae; shelter for birds and insects

**candytufts** *Iberis*
   bees, early-flying butterflies and moths, beetles

**lavenders** *Lavandula*
   flowers attract bees, butterflies, and other insects

**honeysuckles** *Lonicera*
   nectar-rich flowers attract bees, butterflies, and hummingbirds

**honesty** *Lunaria annua*
   annual that feeds butterfly larvae and adults; birds eat seeds

**apples and crabapples** *Malus domestica*
   blossoms attract bees; fruits food for birds and butterflies

**lemon balm, bee balm** *Melissa officialis*
   flowers attract butterflies; ripe spikes attract seed-eating birds

**mints** *Mentha*
   flowers attract butterflies, bees, hover flies, and beneficial insects

**bergamot, bee balm** *Monarda didyma*
   midsummer flowers attract bees and hummingbirds

**coneflowers** *Rudbeckia*
   flowers attract bees and butterflies; birds eat seeds

**sages** *Salvia*
   bees, butterflies, hummingbirds love flowers of different species

**goldenrod** *Solidago*
   bees, butterflies, hoverflies and many other beneficial insects

**stonecrops** *Sedum spectabile*
   bees, butterflies, and almost all late-flying insects

**thymes** *Thymus*
   butterflies, bees, hover flies, and many other insects

**stinging nettles** *Urtica*
   if grown in a sunny place, a butterfly larvae food plant

**verbascums** *Verbascum*
   flowers attract bees; foliage food for moths

may well help the survival of local populations. It is also useful to provide places where butterflies can overwinter. Many species overwinter as eggs, yet several species of fritillaries (*Speyeria*) spend the winter as small caterpillars on violets, while the white butterflies (family *Pieridae*) hibernate in chrysalis form, typically attached to a stem by a silken girdle. This group also includes the charming orange-tip butterfly (*Anthocharis*) and various native whites (*Pontia*), along with the notorious cabbage white (*Artogeia rapae*), an introduced species. All feed on cultivated plants such as cabbage and broccili, but the cabbage white is the bane of vegetable gardeners while the native species are rarely serious pests, particularly if there is a mixed economy of plants and the gardener keeps a wary eye out for the eggs and small larvae that feed on the undersides of leaves.

The monarch butterfly hibernates as an adult in fir forests. It has also colonized places where its main food plant—milkweed—has been introduced into warm-climate gardens, as in the Canary Islands, the Azores, and Australasia.

It is thought that another migratory butterfly that is frequently seen in gardens—the beautiful painted lady, or cosmopolitan butterfly (*Vanessa cardui*)—overwinters as a chrysalis on the edges of deserts. Although neither as big nor as strong a flyer as the monarch, it has been seen up to 2,000 miles (3,000 km) from its winter breeding grounds. It roams widely, feeding on a variety of flowers, including thistles and many other wildflowers. Several generations of this short-lived species may breed during a good summer, with eggs typically laid on thistles, although they also sometimes choose nettles and mallows.

*Opposite* **A path mown through a sea of flowering velvet grass (*Holcus mollis*) in an orchard. Permanent grass is a prime habitat for butterflies and small mammals.**

*Right* **A monarch butterfly (*Danus plexippus*), the largest and most spectacular of migratory butterflies, feeds on the florets of gooseneck loosestrife (*Lysmachia clethroides*). The caterpillar feeds on milkweeds, from which it derives toxins that inhibit most other creatures from eating it.**

# HOW TO MAKE A BIRDHOUSE

Bird conservation organizations have designs for bird houses suitable for different species of bird. Some have entry holes in the front (used by wrens, bluebirds, titmice, or chickadees, depending on size), some are open fronted (for use by robins, barn swallows, or phoebes). A few species prefer side entrances, and hole-nesting owls will sometimes make use of a long, open-topped box, which is sometimes known as a chimney box.

8in (20cm)    10in (25cm)    8in (20cm)    8¼in (21cm)    4in (11cm)    18in (45cm)

6in (15cm)

side    side    front    roof    base    back

This standard birdhouse can be made easily and inexpensively out of a plank of lumber, following a simple cutting plan (*see above*). The pieces are screwed together and an adjustable bit used to drill out the entry/exit hole, the size varying depending on the bird species you wish to attract. The perch can be omitted, since it may encourage predators.

The entry hole in the front should be no more than 1¼in (3.5cm) for wrens, chickadees, and nuthatches. If it is larger, sparrows and starlings will also will be able to use it and are likely to drive away the smaller birds. Woodpeckers may enlarge the entrance for their own use, too. Mice may also set up housekeeping in birdhouses.

2in (5cm)

Hinge the lid with a piece of webbing or tire inner tube. The lid is secured with a galvanized (rustproof) hook and eye. This should discourage some predators. It is better not to peek inside while there are eggs or young.

*Left* Great tit (*Parus major*) feeding its young in a birdhouse. This brood of four is relatively small (5–12 eggs is normal). Great tits and blue tits (*Parus caeruleus*) are common users of birdhouses in Britain.

and it has been shown that suburban birds use lawn far more than comparable areas of arable or natural grassland. Because blackbirds are omnivorous, they also take advantage of bird feeders and fruiting hedges and trees. The blackbird population of gardens in England has been estimated at twenty times that of the surrounding countryside. In Northern American cities, the robin is also extremely populous, especially in urban gardens. It should be remembered, however, that the groundskeeper's "perfect" garden lawn is very heavy on resources as well as pesticides. Less formal lawns that are kept at about 3in (7.5cm) can thrive without artificial fertilizing (and can be cut with a mower with the blade set as high as possible) and, where lawn wildflowers are allowed, make better sense and are more appealing to wildlife. In dry, hot climates it

might be worth using a lawn alternative such as an herb or sedum bed around a flagstone patio or a collection of ornamental grasses.

Longer grass provides shelter for small mammals and larger insects, such as grasshoppers and crickets. The larvae of butterflies, moths, and many other insects can overwinter on grasses and other wild plants. Some butterfly species are conservative about where they lay their eggs, and a large garden that has an area set aside as long grass (an orchard, for example) can be of significant conservation value. It is better to let grass grow naturally in an orchard, since fruit trees suffer from competition with close-mown grass. The seed heads of grassland plants are also an important food source. Ants' nests in long grass provide an extra incentive for woodpeckers to visit the garden.

*Above* Birdhouses should be placed where predators will have trouble reaching them. The design and height above ground of the house should be appropriate for the species you are trying to attract. With a 3in (7.5cm) hole, this house, situated in an oak tree, might attract a screech owl, or if the entrance hole were to be smaller (1–1½/3–4cm), some house wrens.

Birds, especially finches, also appreciate garden plants that produce large seed heads. The affinity of finches for the thistle family (including many garden-worthy ones) is well known; they also love sunflowers. Yarrow (*Alchemilla millifolium*), globe thistle (*Echinops ritro*), goldenrod (*Solidago*), rose campion (*Lychnis coronaria*), coneflowers (*Echinacea* and *Rudbeckia*), and chicory (*Cichorium intybus*) are all plants that produce attractive flowers and good seed. Birds are the most visible seed eaters, but other animals such as ants and beetles appreciate them as well, taking the seeds away as soon as they have fallen. Indeed, ants are responsible for sowing and spreading a number of plant species.

Trees give shelter, nesting places, and food for birds. Insects and other invertebrates live in crevices in the bark, and insectivorous birds will feed on them. In open places, trunks and branches are also colonized by lichens that will provide food for a microfauna and do the trees no harm at all. Flowering trees and shrubs give nectar for birds and insects, and berries and other fruits from late

summer through to winter. Buddleja, which has spread to naturalize in many places throughout the world, is a marvelously rich source of nectar and seed, attracting an incredible diversity of butterflies, moths, bees, wasps, lacewings, and other insects. Extra nesting places can be provided by putting up birdhouses, although care has to be taken with siting, since many predators can also climb or fly.

Hedges and coniferous trees with dense foliage give shelter and nesting sites to birds and are particularly significant for small birds that have difficulty in keeping warm in hard winters. Butterflies may also roost in hedges, although walls draped by vines are even more useful.

Some birds may nest in holes and crevices in walls that are covered by foliage, notably wrens and robins in the lower reaches, and flycatchers at higher levels. Climbing plants can be a great boon for wildlife as well as a joy to gardeners. A vast diversity of invertebrate life also thrives in the damp shade on and within walls, including sow bugs, spiders, beetles, and ants. Bird houses securely placed on walls are generally safer for the inhabitants than those in trees, although they should not be sited in direct sunlight.

Finally, you should not forget the soil itself. In an organically rich garden soil, huge numbers of tiny and microscopic creatures are actively busy. We are familiar with the larger ones, such as earthworms, slugs, snails, centipedes, millipedes, spiders, sow bugs, ants, and beetles, but while we know the names of most of our garden birds there are few gardeners who can distinguish one sow bug from another or have any idea of the identity of the thousands of different beetles. The microorganisms exist in countless billions, recycling the organic matter in the soil. One group in particular is responsible for the sweet smell of good soil and well-made compost. Attempting to single out friend and foe is a largely unrewarding task—it is preferable to add well-rotted garden compost and other humus-rich materials and to grow a mixture of plants that thrive in their selected positions in order to promote a natural balance.

*Below* **This open-fronted birdhouse is stuffed with hollow plant stems. Tucked away within the ivy, they present a sheltered site where overwintering insects can shelter comfortably. The scheme is evidently a success, because this house has at least five occupants.**

# HOW TO MAKE A BAT HOUSE

Bat houses are not quite so successful with their intended residents as garden birdhouses, but it is well worth the effort of putting a few in place, because bats are such delightful creatures. Bats suffer from lack of habitat, so bat houses in suitable gardens can be extremely valuable. Because most bats move roosts fairly frequently, your bat house will probably not have full-time occupation, but do not disturb it through curiosity.

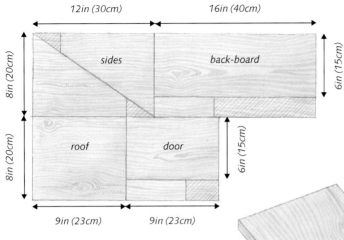

1 This house, known as the "Tanglewood Wedge" house, is of simple construction if you follow the cutting plan (*see above*). It is not insulated, so it serves as a daytime roost between late spring and autumn. The wood should be left rough and untreated.

2 Glue as well as screw the wood pieces together to make the box less drafty. Use an odor-free glue, otherwise the bats will stay away. Make the entrance slit as wide as an adult finger.

3 It is best to position bat houses as high up in a tree as possible (at least 16ft/5m), since bats prefer to roost high. Face them southwest, southeast, or north, so that the house catches some sun but does not bake. Put two or three houses side by side on a tree.

*Left* The bat house position should not be too exposed, but the flight path to it should be unimpeded. The wood will weather, so the houses will quickly become part of the scenery. If there is no sign of occupancy (such as droppings on the batten step or through direct observation) after a year or so, move the boxes to another site.

*There is something special about eating out of doors, particularly in the easy informality that a natural style confers on a garden. A table with chairs can be a semipermanent fixture, while a bench in the sun by the back door provides a place to open mail or to prepare vegetables. There is also a need for occasional chairs, benches, and cushions that can be taken into private shade, for quiet contemplation on your own or for teenagers to find a secluded spot to hide away.*

*Opposite* **A tree house is a dream for almost every child—and indeed for many adults. This house is sturdy, high, and brand new. As it ages, it will weather to the shade of the ash tree in which it is lodged. When making a tree house, it is important to make sure the ladder is safe and securely fitted.**

# Leisure in the garden

A garden in which the plants have a certain autonomy is forever changing and will always be interesting. There is invariably a plant coming into flower, or something that is so stunningly at its peak that it stops you in your tracks. The pure refreshment of stepping outside, even if just for a few moments, letting your attention wander and soaking in the atmosphere is a simple tonic that should not be overlooked. For children, gardens are secret places, where they can investigate scents and sounds, taking in their impressions, so that later in life the perfume of a particular rose, the tang of privet flower, or a bird's song will transport them back to childhood.

While you should provide play places for children, it is equally—if not more—important to allow them to find their own way around the garden. They may like to sleep in the long grass, make daisy chains on the lawn, hide in arbors, make castles of large fallen trunks, climb trees (there are few more enjoyable pastimes than sitting hidden in the branches of a tree, with an apple and a favorite cat). Some children like to grow things, but often this is something that comes with age and to force the pace can put them off. Most children, however, like eating, and to give children a strawberry patch, a plum or apple tree, or a fruit bush that is their very own and from which they can pick their own fruit can be the start of a lifelong affinity both for the garden and for healthy eating.

*Left* **A small bed containing something delicious, such as strawberries, may draw children to the garden better than a decorative bed. They may especially enjoy picking ripe strawberries.**

# Play in the garden

Play in the garden is not confined to the younger age group. Swings should be strong enough to support an adult (a Watteau fantasy is open to anyone), and a large seesaw is as inviting to grown-ups as to children. Secure a long plank between two heavy metal wheels, and you can move it to prevent wear being concentrated in one place.

Swings are lovely things to have in a garden and help children to develop a good sense of balance. The simplest and often the most enjoyed kind can be made by hanging a car tire securely from a strong branch of a tree. It makes for good fun if the children can then swing over a stream or ditch. A straightforward flat-platform swing can also be

hung from a tree, but if you have no trees suitable or large enough most stores sell them with free-standing supports. To be safe, the supports must be firmly secured, preferably sunk in a concrete base. A thick layer of chipped bark beneath makes a soft landing and saves the mess and mud that occurs when the grass wears thin.

If you live in the country or have access to tree trunks, consider importing some to your garden. Having their own rustic seat in a quiet place or a "tree trunk throne" appeals to most children.

There is, of course, a great deal of difference between the desires of toddlers, teenage children, and adults, let alone the different needs of all the

*Above* **A rough-hewn two-seater throne seat with a luxuriant canopy of common English ivy (*Hedera helix*). A floral element is supplied by the hardy cranesbill (*Geranium*) and the fleshy stonecrop (*Sedum*) growing on either side of the throne.**

*Left* **Swings need to be securely fitted. The structure can be something of an eyesore, however, so here the structural poles are swathed with climbing roses. Adults can go on enjoying this particular swing after the children have grown up, or just allow it to be used as a trellis for the roses.**

# HOW TO MAKE GARDEN FURNITURE

Tree trunks from your own or your friends' felled trees can be used to make garden furniture that fits suitably into a natural-style garden. The trunks will have to be sound and fairly large. You will need a chainsaw to make this furniture, but if you are not used to operating one of these powered machines, it is wiser— and much safer—to find someone with experience who could do the job for you.

## BASIC UNIT
This unit consists simply of a section of trunk with a niche cut out of it and the base leveled so that it cannot roll. For extra stability it can be partly dug into the ground. It should be quite solid, the total width at least twice as wide as the niche cut for the crosspiece.

*cross section through two saddles*

## SEESAW
This seesaw consists of a basic unit and rocker seat. Instead of a normal plank, you can substitute a tree trunk with niche seats cut at either end on the surface that will be the upper part of the seesaw. Cut a saddle underneath in two centers of the lower surface. This should fit fairly snugly into the saddle in the basic unit, to prevent the seesaw from shifting or swaying.

## THRONE SEAT
This rustic chair could not be simpler. Cut an L-shape from a log, making the seat higher or lower depending on whom it is intended for. If the seat is to be positioned on uneven ground, dig a flat hole for its base in the ground to secure it.

## BENCH
The rustic bench calls for two basic units and a log cut in two down the center, with two saddles that slot into those of the basic units. Ensure that the bench is comfortable and correctly balanced, cut the niches to exactly the same depth as for the basic units. If you have two logs to work with, you can make two matching benches, using one log for the four basic units; the other log divided in two makes the two flat-topped seats. This style of rustic furniture will weather with the years, but even when made out of poor-quality timber it should last for a long while.

individuals involved. You can't please everybody, but if I can generalize it is true to say that children have a kind of recognition of good places, just as wild creatures do. Create a garden that has a natural flow in which the plants and wildlife thrive, and there is a pretty good chance that all age groups will find a niche that will match their moods and needs. It is up to you to maintain the diversity, then leave it to them to choose.

Larger gardens can afford space for a place to play catch, but if space is at a premium, a spring meadow can be rough-mown a few weeks after flowering to provide room during the summer and fall. A basketball net takes up so little room it could fit into almost any garden.

A natural garden should attract a wide range of bird life, and observations of unusual species or regular census studies can be of great help to bird conservation organizations. If your research is more casual and sporadic, make a garden bird chart to remind you to record those that have come into the garden. Use different marks for birds seen flying over the garden, including passing migrants; birds that have actually come into the garden; and birds that have bred in the garden. Parents who start this as a project for their children often end up continuing after their offspring have grown up and left home. Children find a pleasure in learning how to observe and identify birds that may last them for the rest of their lives.

## Seasonal observations

The Chinese have a game called "looking for spring" in which they search for the first signs of reawakening life. These might include a bird breaking into song or the first buds appearing after winter, the first break of blossom or agitation among winter migrant birds. It is a cheerful game and can be carried out anywhere.

Summer is a good time for doing bird observations: a garden census, for example, or a detailed study of one birdhouse. It has been estimated that blue tit parents need to find something like 15,000 caterpillars in order to raise a single brood. Other members of the tit and chickadee group have similar requirements. That

*Right* **A dwarf apple tree heavily laden with fruit. The dwarfing rootstock limits growth to manageable proportions for a small garden. The apple is the familiar 'Golden Delicious,' which, when grown in good organic soil and picked at the right moment, actually does live up to its name.**

amount of caterpillars represents many trips to and from the nest. When do the parents start? Do they get the food nearby? Is it nearby? Count the trips they make in five minutes? If you watch carefully and are lucky, you may even be fortunate enough to see the baby birds coming out to fly for the first time.

Autumn is usually a good period for observing spiders. How many different kinds inhabit the garden? Do they all have webs? What is the geometry of an orb web? Do spiders fly? Try bringing a trowel full of leaf litter indoors. Put it on a tray and look through a hand lens or magnifying glass, for it will come to life after a few minutes. At a conservative estimate, it could contain earthworms and slugs, millipedes, insects and insect larvae, sow bugs, and spiders. A microscope would highlight quantities of microfauna, microfungi, and millions of bacteria. All these are necessary to complete the process of recycling the leaves and other dead and dying organic matter.

If winter brings snow, any tracks are intriguing. You may find animals in the garden you never guessed were there. Look for cones and nuts: You can tell what has been eating them by the pattern of bites, nibbles, or beak blows. There is also the puzzle of where insects go in winter. The complete life cycle of even quite-familiar garden insects is not fully known or understood, yet the birds know where to find them. You can see birds working their way along branches (sometimes while they are awaiting their turn at the feeder) and down the rough bark of trunks, as well as in crevices in walls, where they can find concealed insects and bugs.

### Found objects in the garden

I am always surprised by the sheer number of things of interest to be discovered in a garden. Items that are dug up in the course of cultivating the ground can be fascinating, and in older gardens can yield a trail of history. Among the objects found

*Above* **You need to have a large garden with some water if you want to keep ducks, but they are most friendly and rewarding creatures. This motley little domestic flock includes Aylesburies, hybrid mallards, tufted ducks, and mandarins. It is essential to shut them up in a secure shed at night or they may be eaten by foxes.**

by our family and friends are fossils, carved flints, clay pipe stems and bowls, and antique bottles and pots. More numerous are pieces of crockery, rusted knives, and other kitchen implements. The shape, quality, and patterning of the pottery can be interesting, but rusted metal should be treated with caution. A local history society or museum may be able to help with the identification of many of the objects. The most interesting items can be assembled and labeled and made into an extemporary garden museum.

### Pets

As they get older, many children yearn for pets. The foremost principle here should be that an animal is an individual in its own right and not an animated cuddly toy, and that all animals need appropriate attention and places to live. Animal welfare organizations will advise on the needs and care of pet animals. Some animals, especially those used to living alongside humans such as cats and dogs, do not fret at close contact with people, and these make the most rewarding pets. For many years our family enjoyed keeping ducks, and as far as we could tell the ducks liked us, but you need to be able to provide water and a separate pen or the run of an orchard, since ducks are no respecters of plant life. There is a domestic breed called Khaki Campbell that is very tame and easily domesticated. They are regular layers but seem to lack an instinct for brooding so do not appear to mind when you gather the eggs. It is, however, essential to shut them in a secure shed at dusk, because foxes and other predators are quick to take advantage of animals whose natural defenses and sense of fear have been bred out of them.

### Garden safety

A disturbing number of accidents seem to happen in gardens. Some are inevitable. There are jobs you think you can just fit into a small amount of time, and then you can not find your goggles or boots. There is considerable temptation simply to get on with the task rather than spend a quarter of an hour looking for a missing item.

It is easy to be lazy about safety, but wise gardeners will use iron self-discipline to train themselves into the habit of mind that resembles that of a trained horticultural worker. One of the problems for the garden owner is that there is a multiplicity of jobs demanding different skills, none of which are done frequently enough to achieve a real level of skill and competence.

In some cases, you do not recognize danger, until after the event. I have partially toed friends who mowed uneven ground in soft shoes, using a rotary mower that spun out of control. I have come across adults, and one sad case of a child, who suffered terribly from skin blistering equivalent to second-and third-degree burns after cutting back undergrowth that included the umbellifers, principally the giant hogweed (*Heracleum mantegazzianum*) but also cow parsnip (*H. spondylium*). Shorts and thong sandals are utterly inappropriate for tasks such as these.

*Below* **Autumn is the time for spiders' webs. The dew and sunlight catch the beauty of an orb spider web and several woolly hammocks made by funnel spiders. The webs are slung on the twigs of barberries and roses, but spiders are not choosy—any dense shrub will suit them.**

Everyday plants such as hawthorns, pyracanthas, roses, and brambles can inflict unpleasant gashes and wounds on the unwary. It is necessary to remember that maintenance means clearing or pruning, damaging, uprooting, chopping back, or even killing these plants. Plants cannot run away, so they have other means of defending themselves, and it is foolish not to recognize this and clothe yourself accordingly. If you have planned your garden well, such jobs should be minimized. It is better, for example, to plant a shrub that will grow to fit a space when fully mature than to put in some large and vigorous plant that forces you into doing battle with it several times a year.

## Minimizing risk

Even a garden that aspires to a natural style will need a certain amount of maintenance, and it is sensible to accord your plants the courtesy of respect. Minimizing risk involves assessing and reducing danger at early stages in a project.

*Above* **An outdoor display of shells, in this case marine species. Similar displays could be made with fossils, pieces of clay pipe and other historic artifacts, or with different-sized and -colored snail shells.**

*Left* **An ingenious basket sculpture that can be refilled with different collections of pine cones, leaves, shells, twigs, or pebbles arranged in varying patterns. It could also be moved physically to a different part of the garden to make a change or to mark different seasons.**

*Above* **This fine collection of old wooden tools is almost a horticultural museum exhibit, but they are all still used. You can buy modern tools that are equally attractive and useful. The multinational nature of contemporary trade also means that we can sample interesting tools from many countries.**

avoid a danger (such as poisonous plants) is better than having the danger lifted out of the way. In the end, the safest course of action is for adujlts to be with children as much as possible when they are in the garden, and to reinforce the safety requirements when an appropriate situation arises.

Of course, there are precautions that should always be taken, for yourselves as adults as well as for children. Electrically powered tools, for example, should always be plugged into a grounded circuit that has a circuit breaker. Long extension cords are a hazard, particularly in large gardens and when children are around, since many feet of cable may be out of sight. Battery-powered tools may be preferable in these circumstances. The technology of battery-powered tools, such as hedge trimmers, is developing fast, and light, efficient models that are easy to use are now available.

With any power equipment—electric, battery, or gas—goggles are essential. It is far too easy for a chip of wood, a piece of dirt, or a twig to fly up from clippers or a mower and get into an eye. Eye and hearing protection must always be used when shredders are working.

### Ergonomic tools

It is a good idea to use tools that feel good in your hands and that you can operate comfortably and efficiently. This applies to hand tools as much as to powered ones. It is stupid to be straining to dig out a plant with a fork, and levering your back into all kinds of disadvantageous positions, when you would do better using a mattock, which has more leverage for less power. Nowadays, a wide range of well-made tools are available, some of them borrowed from other countries and cultures. It may well be that because of your size and build you would be better off with a long-handled Italian spade or a Vietnamese hoe than the standard designs prevalent in North America.

Sturdy top-of-the-line tools are always a good investment. Such well-made tools may cost a bit more than their poorly made counterparts, but they generally do their job more efficiently and easily.

Some designs—slippery steps, for example—are inherently dangerous. You may decide to keep them for aesthetic or other reasons, but you must always be aware on your own behalf and you must warn others who frequent the garden, too.

Some parents like to have a direct sightline right along the garden to the places where their children are likely to play. This is a good idea as long as the children conform to expectations, but many of the problems occur when they do not. One thing that is emphasized less than it could be in regard to child safety is to warn children properly. Clearly, with some children this represents a challenge, but if warnings are heeded, being able to recognize and

## HOW TO MAKE A PEBBLE POOL

A ground-level pebble pool is safe for children because there is no standing water. The water from the fountain drains through the pebbles back into the reservoir below. The layer of pebbles rests on a piece of heavy wire mesh, which is supported by a 3in (8cm) ledge. This is also a good design for introducing water into a small garden, because the pebbles can take up as little as 24in (60cm) in diameter. Wind and evaporation cause some water loss, but apart from filling up the reservoir regularly, this design needs little maintenance.

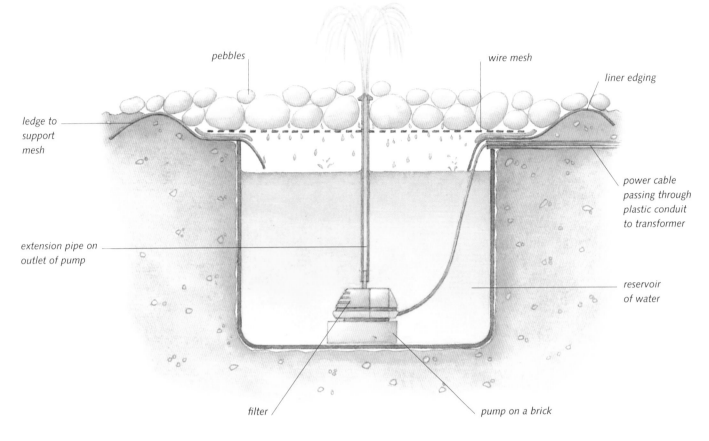

*pebbles*

*wire mesh*

*liner edging*

*ledge to support mesh*

*power cable passing through plastic conduit to transformer*

*extension pipe on outlet of pump*

*reservoir of water*

*filter*

*pump on a brick*

*Left* This pebble-lined pool is different from the illustration above in that it has an accessible water reservoir, which means it would be unsafe for young children. It is made by covering a butyl-lined standard pool with a quantity of large pebbles. This kind of pool would probably look best in a coastal garden.

A stable natural ecosystem maintains itself in what is described as a dynamic equilibrium; that means that even though there are changes, depending on climate and weather and the internal growth and decay within the system, the ecosystem keeps itself pretty much in balance. A garden that borrows a natural style does not have this inherent stability, and the gardener's task is to restore equilibrium if some plants seem to be getting too much out of hand and to maintain a positive interactive cycle between people and plants.

*Opposite* **A rich mixture of loose-knit, naturalistic planting in wonderful health in an organic garden. The rose 'New Dawn' makes a backdrop with the rose 'Constance Spry,' with golden hop growing in front of it and tall royal blue anchusa, yellow *Anthemis tinctoria* 'Iden,' *Erysimum* 'Bowles Mauve' starting to seed, and bronze fennel just beginning to become bushy.**

# The natural cycle

The principle is to learn from natural systems and to reinterpret them for the garden. It is important to keep in mind that you are dealing with a garden rather than a piece of wilderness and that you yourself are part of the living system.

In the wild, natural cycles of decomposition keep the soil fertile. Soil organic matter is constantly replenished as plant and animal debris decomposes. In the garden, you fuel this natural process: Maintenance in the garden produces organic debris in the form of prunings, surplus plants, leaves, and weeds. Mix this organic matter with waste from the kitchen to make compost—a fast-track version of natural recycling. Once the organic matter has broken down into compost, it can be returned to the garden where it is needed. Making compost is easy once you have established a routine—a bucket for scraps in the kitchen and an out-of-the-way spot in the garden for collecting and mixing. Once the materials are combined, the compost basically makes itself. I also use natural liquid seaweed and seaweed meal for improving soil fertility and feeding plants.

*Left* **Lemon balm (*Melissa officinalis*), purple sage (*Salvia officinalis* 'Purpurescens'), common thyme (*Thymus vulgaris*), and parsley (*Petroselinum crispum*) are here growing in a crisp group with delightful contrasts of color and texture.**

## COLLECTING AND DRYING SEED

Seed may be derived from a number of sources. Gathering the seed from your own garden is the most convenient, because you can wait for the moment when it is precisely ripe. If friends offer seed from their gardens, you may find that it is slightly underripe. Put the seed heads or fruits into an envelope or paper bag and start the storage procedure as soon as you get home. When gathering seed from the wild, make sure it is ripe and collect judiciously, leaving plenty of seeds where you found them. Any seed that is not to be used at once should be stored in a cool, dark place.

1 Gather the ripe pods, capsules, or fruits—love-in-a-mist (*Nigella damascena*) is shown here—in the afternoon, when the early dews have dried away. Spread on a piece of paper towel, laid on a seed flat set in a warm place to dry further, if necessary.

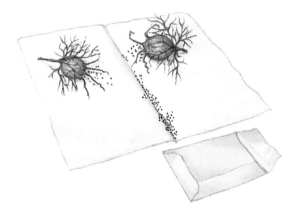

2 Make sure you distinguish seeds from bits of seed case or pod. Gently empty all the seeds onto a sheet of white paper. Remove any that look underripe or are damaged; tip the rest into a small paper envelope, on which you should write the name of the plant, where it was collected, and the date.

Underwater tanks are also used as larger reservoirs that are capacious, cool, and hidden out of sight. A small pump, such as the ones used in garden ponds, can be fitted to bring up the water when it is needed.

### Seeds and seedlings

The natural garden, with its emphasis on plants that self-seed and naturalize, needs a special touch when it comes to new plants. Seedlings should be cherished, which means that garden hoes can be discarded in favor of tools that allow the gardener to be more discriminating.

Self-sown seedlings sometimes grow in the most fortuitous places, creating effects you could not have dreamed of. They also get themselves into totally awkward situations—growing through a doormat, blocking a fall of steps, or simply looking out of place in the overall design of the garden. These will have to be removed from their original

*Left* Mullein (*Verbascum phoeniceum*), growing with hostas, a light purple form of wild pansy (*Viola tricolor*), and the simple, short blue spires of bugleweed (*Ajuga reptans*) in a quiet corner of the garden. This combination of perennials and self-seeders is especially attractive, because it will more or less take care of itself, with a minimum of care.

place and be transplanted to a good site. Complete this procedure as quickly as possible and water in the transplant with dilute seaweed.

## Recycling within the garden

The aim of a garden in a natural style is to be as self-sustaining as possible. A woodland-edge area of the garden will have its own leaf fall, although it can also be enriched by applications of leaf mold. This can be turned into the soil during weeding, and placed around plants such as hellebores and hardy geraniums in early spring, when new growth is just beginning to show.

Compost is welcome almost anywhere but especially in prairie borders, mixed beds, and places where you grow vegetables and fruit. If there is any to spare, a raked and spiked lawn will enjoy the tonic of compost lightly sprinkled over it in autumn. (Dried seaweed can also be used as a topdressing in spring or autumn.) Hot, dry beds will benefit from any additional compost worked into their soil. It is easy to forget that hedges like an application of compost or manure at their base every few years, the frequency depending on the health and vigor of the hedge. It is beneficial to apply manure or compost after a hedge has been hard pruned.

Comparative trials recently carried out in Britain with a range of identical plants showed that most plants grew and flowered extremely well without the application of artificial fertilizers—indeed some actually did better. Lavender, which is known to prefer a dry, well-drained, poor soil, did marvelously in the unfertilized plot, as would be expected, but roses, grasses, and Chilean glory flower (*Eccremocarpus scaber*) exceeded all expectations and flowered prolifically. As well as lavenders, shrubs such as broom, buddleja, California lilac (*Ceanothus*), and rosemary actually seem to thrive more in a poor soil. Annuals such as California poppies (*Eschscholzia californica*), cosmos, and viper's bugloss (*Echium*) also seem to do well and flower earlier in poorer soil. Meadow plants do not like improved soil, so you should mow any meadow area after the plants have

flowered and then rake off the grass clippings. It seems to be best if the meadow flowers are allowed to seed some, but not all, years.

Prairie borders, which do not have a grass matrix and where the plants are more densely planted, benefit from compost or leaf mold applied in spring. It is also worth remembering that while weeds can get established in a rich organic soil, it is much easier to pull them out. Even really difficult weeds with deep, interconnecting strings of roots, such as quackgrass and bindweeds, come out quite readily in a good soil.

*Above* **Too wild for some tastes—a tumble of annual and perennial plants, and lumps of purple loosestrife (*Lythrum salicaria*), grasses, and shrubs, interspersed with blue buttons (*Knautia arvensis*) and self-seeded annuals, such as the common poppy (*Papaver rhoeas*) and borage (*Borago officinalis*).**

# Plant and habitat guide

These tables summarize some of the practical characteristics of a selection of plants suitable for the habitats mentioned in this book. Take this as a starting point and use another guide, such as a plant encyclopedia, to fill out the detail. Remember that no plant is entirely typical, and there will always be surprises when plants begin growing in your own garden.

**KEY**

❋ plant can withstand temperatures down to 20°F

❋❋ plant can withstand temperatures down to -20°F

❋❋❋ plant can withstand temperatures down to -40°F

**ESp** *Early Spring*  **Su** *Summer*
**Sp** *Spring*  **LSu** *Late Summer*
**LSp** *Late Spring*  **Au** *Autumn*
**ESu** *Early Summer*  **LAu** *Late Autumn*

| BOTANICAL NAME | HEIGHT AND SPREAD | DESCRIPTION | SEASON | ZONES | HARDINESS | ORIGIN |
|---|---|---|---|---|---|---|
| **HOT, DRY PLACES** | | | | | | |
| **SHRUBS** | | | | | | |
| Artemisia 'Powis Castle' | H2ft/60cm S16–32in/40–80cm | Evergreen feathery, silvery foliage | Su | 5–8 | ❋❋ | Mediterranean |
| Caryopteris x clandonensis | H3ft/1m S5ft/1.5m | Clusters of small purple-blue flowers; gray-green leaves | Su | 6–9 | ❋ | Asia |
| Cotoneaster horizontalis | H2–3ft/60–90cm S4–8ft/1.2–2.5m | Evergreen/semievergreen; white spring flowers; red summer-to-fall fruit | Sp/A | 4–7 | ❋❋ | China |
| Euphorbia characias subsp. characias | H/S4ft/1.2m | Evergreen dense bluish foliage; rich lime-green heads | Sp | 7–9 | ❋ | Mediterranean |
| Lavandula angustifolia 'Hidcote' | H24in/60cm S30in/75cm | Evergreen compact, gray-green foliage; deep purple flowers | Su | 5–8 | ❋❋ | Mediterranean |
| Perovskia atriplicifolia 'Blue Spire' | H/S4ft/1.2m | Russian sage; misty spires of violet-blue flowers; gray-green foliage | LSu | 4–9 | ❋❋ | Central Asia |
| **PERENNIALS AND BULBS** | | | | | | |
| Canna indica | H6ft/2m S20in/50cm | Tender perennial grown as an annual; bright-flowered rhizomatous plant | Su | 8–11 | ❋ | Asia, Americas |
| Coreopsis verticillata 'Moonbeam' | H20in/50cm S12in/30cm | Feathery dark leaves; yellow flowers | Su | 3–9 | ❋❋❋ | Maryland–N.Carolina |
| Eryngium x tripartitum | H24in/60cm S20in/50cm | Spiny blue-green thistle with small violet flower heads on branched stems | Su | 5–8 | ❋❋ | Mediterranean |
| Gaura lindheimeri | H32in/80cm S35in/90cm | Graceful plant with white pink-tinged butterflylike flowers | LSu | 5–9 | ❋❋ | Texas/Louisiana |
| Verbascum chaixii | H2–3ft/60–90cm S20in/50cm | Branched spikes of yellow or white flowers | Su | 4–8 | ❋❋ | Europe |
| Yucca filamentosa | H3ft/90cm S5ft/1.5m | Evergreen; spikes of white flowers; strap-shaped green or variegated leaves | Su | 3–10 | ❋❋❋ | E. USA |

*Canna indica*

*Eschscholzia californica*

*Rosa x odorata 'Mutabilis'*

| BOTANICAL NAME | HEIGHT AND SPREAD | DESCRIPTION | SEASON | ZONES | HARDINESS | ORIGIN |
|---|---|---|---|---|---|---|
| **WALL AND PAVING CREVICES** | | | | | | |
| *Antennaria dioica* | H2in/5cm S6in/15cm | Semievergreen; clusters of white or pale pink flowers; gray-green leaves | Sp/Su | 5–9 | ✼✼ | Europe, N. Asia, N. America |
| *Phlox subulata* | H2–6in/5–15cm S20in/50cm | Evergreen mats of purple, pink, or white flowers; needlelike leaves | ESp | 3–8 | ✼✼✼ | E. & C. USA |
| *Sempervivum* species | H1–6in/2.5–15cm S20in/50cm | Evergreen; red-purple flowers; rosettes of maroon-green or silver foliage | Su | 4–9 | ✼✼ | Europe |
| *Thymus pulegioides* | H2–10in/5–25cm S12in/30cm | Aromatic small leaves; pink-purple whorled flowers | ESu | 4–9 | ✼✼ | Europe |
| **ANNUALS** | | | | | | |
| *Argyranthemum frutescens* | H/S32in/80cm | Tender perennial grown as an annual; daisy flowers; feathery foliage | Su | | | Canary Islands |
| *Eschscholzia californica* | H12in/30cm S6in/15cm | Bright, silky-textured poppies | Su | | | W. USA |

## SHADY PLACES

| | | | | | | |
|---|---|---|---|---|---|---|
| **TREES AND SHRUBS** | | | | | | |
| *Cercis canadensis* | H/S30ft/10m | Redbud; masses of tiny pink flowers; heart-shaped leaves | ESp/ Sp | 5–9 | ✼✼ | N. America |
| *Cornus mas* | H/S15ft/5m | Cornelian cherry; clusters of tiny yellow flowers; red summer fruit | ESp | 5–8 | ✼✼ | Europe, W. Asia |
| *Hydrangea quercifolia* | H6ft/2m S8ft/2.5m | Oakleaf hydrangea; trusses of white flowers; large leaves; good fall color | Su/A | 5–9 | ✼✼ | S.E. USA |
| *Rhododendron schlippenbachii* | H/S15ft/5m | Royal azalea; clusters of pale pink to white flowers | Sp | 5–8 | ✼✼ | China, Korea |
| *Rosa x odorata* 'Mutabilis' | H3ft/90cm S2ft/60cm | Changing honey, pink, or orange single flowers; good in poor soil | All | 6–9 | ✼ | China |
| *Sarcococca hookeriana* | H/S5ft/1.5m | Suckering evergreen; fragrant white flowers; black fruit | Sp | 6–9 | ✼ | W. China |
| **VINES** | | | | | | |
| *Clematis montana* | H23ft/7m S10ft/3m | Good for shaded walls, poor soils; scented; will grow into trees | ESu | 6–9 | ✼ | China |
| *Hedera helix* | H/S 4–10ft/1.2–3m | English ivy; evergreen foliage plant | All | 6–9 | ✼ | Europe |
| *Humulus lupulus* 'Aureus' | H/S 20ft/6m | Hops; deeply cut golden-yellow foliage | Su/A | 4–8 | ✼✼ | Eu, Asia, N. America |
| *Hydrangea anomala* subsp. *petiolaris* | H 50ft/14m S20ft/6m | Climbing hydrangea; white flower clusters; handsome flaking bark | ESu | 4–9 | ✼✼ | Russia, Asia |
| *Parthenocissus tricuspidata* | H 50ft/14m S20ft/6m | Boston ivy; toothed lobed leaves with brilliant red fall color | Su/A | 4–8 | ✼✼ | China, Korea, Japan |
| *Schizophragma hydrangeoides* | H40ft/12m S20ft/6m | Japanese hydrangea vine; flattened clusters of creamy flowers | Su | 6–9 | ✼ | Japan, Korea |
| **GROUNDCOVERS** | | | | | | |
| *Ajuga reptans* | H6in/15cm S2–3ft/60–90cm | Bugleweed; evergreen/semievergreen; spikes of purple-blue flowers | Sp/Su | 3–9 | ✼✼✼ | Europe, N. Africa |
| *Asarum europaeum* | H3in/7.5cm S12in/30cm | European wild ginger; evergreen; insignificant brown flowers; glossy leaves | All | 4–8 | ✼✼ | W. Europe |
| *Campanula portenschlagiana* | H6in/15cm S2ft/60cm | Dalmation bellflower; small lavender bells; bright heart-shaped leaves | Su | 4–7 | ✼✼ | E Europe |
| *Dicentra eximia* | H/S 18–24in/45–60cm | Fringed bleeding heart; sprays of pink or white flowers; fernlike foliage | LSp/ Su | 4–8 | ✼✼ | E. USA |
| *Helleborus x hybridus* | H/S18–24in/45–60cm | Lenten rose; evergreen; glossy leaves | All | 4–9 | ✼✼ | garden origin |

| BOTANICAL NAME | HEIGHT AND SPREAD | DESCRIPTION | SEASON | ZONES | HARDINESS | ORIGIN |
|---|---|---|---|---|---|---|
| **FERNS** | | | | | | |
| *Asplenium trichomanes* | H6in/15cm S8in/20cm | Maidenhair spleenwort; evergreen/ semievergreen with wiry black stalks | All | 5–8 | ✳✳ | subcosmopolitan |
| *Athyrium niponicum* | H 8–12in/20–30in S2–3ft/60–90cm | Japanese painted fern; fronds marked with silver, maroon, and green | All | 5–8 | ✳✳ | Japan |
| *Polystichum acrostichoides* | H18in/45cm S36in/90cm | Christmas fern; evergreen; clumps of dark green featherlike fronds with small spiny pinnae | All | 3–8 | ✳✳✳ | N.E. N. America |

## MEADOWS AND PRAIRIES

### LOW MEADOWS

| | | | | | | |
|---|---|---|---|---|---|---|
| *Bellis perennis* | H/S2–8in/5–20cm | Daisy; small daisy flowers; commonly grown as an annual | Sp | 4–8 | ✳✳ | Europe, N. America |
| *Crocus* species | H2–4in/5–10cm | White, rose-purple, violet, or yellow flowers; self-sows in suitable sites | ESp | 3–8 | ✳✳✳ | S. Europe, N. Africa |
| *Eranthis hyemalis* | H2–3in/5–8cm S2in/5cm | Winter aconite; yellow flowers | ESp | 4–9 | ✳✳ | S.E. Europe |
| *Fritillaria meleagris* | H6–12in/15–30cm S3in/8cm | Checkered lily; red (or white) bell-shaped, pendent flowers | Sp | 3–8 | ✳✳✳ | Europe |
| *Hyacinthoides hispanica* | H16in/40cm S24in/60cm+ | Spanish bluebells; erect spikes of bell-shaped blue, pink, or white flowers | S/LSp | 4–9 | ✳✳ | S.E. Europe, N. Africa |
| *Iris reticulata* | H4–6in/10–15cm | Reticulated iris; violet to purple-blue flowers; grasslike leaves | ESp | 5–8 | ✳✳ | S. Europe, N. Africa |
| *Primula veris* | H/S10in/25cm | Cowslip; yellow nodding flowers | LSp | 3–8 | ✳✳✳ | Europe–W. Asia |
| *Primula vulgaris* | H8in/20cm S12in/30cm | Primrose; yellow-rosetted flowers | Sp | 4–8 | ✳✳ | Eurasia |
| *Prunella vulgaris* | H6in/15cm S3ft/90cm | Self-heal; erect spikes of tiny pinkish-purple flowers | Su | 5–8 | ✳✳ | S.E. Europe |
| *Scilla bifolia* | H2–8in/5–20cm S1in/3cm | Squill; small bulbous perennial; deep blue flowers | Sp | 3–8 | ✳✳✳ | S., C., & E. Europe |
| *Veronica chamaedrys* | H3–6in/8–15cm S6–20in/15–50cm | Germander speedwell; sky-blue twinkling flowers; naturalized N. America | Sp/Su | 3–7 | ✳✳✳ | Europe |
| *Vicia cracca* | H/S5ft/1.5m | Tufted vetch; scrambling or climbing blue-flowered perennial | Su | 3–7 | ✳✳✳ | Eurasia |

### SUMMER MEADOWS

| | | | | | | |
|---|---|---|---|---|---|---|
| *Achillea millefolium* | H8–12in/15–30cm S12in/30cm | Yarrow; white flowers in flat heads | Su | 3–9 | ✳✳✳ | widespread |
| *Asclepias tuberosa* | H3ft/90cm S12in/30cm | Butterfly weed; clusters of small orange-red flowers; attracts butterflies | Su | 4–9 | ✳✳ | N. America |
| *Cichorium intybus* | H4ft/1.2m S2ft/60cm | Chicory; clear blue flowers | Su | 4–8 | ✳✳ | Mediterranean |
| *Daucus carota* | H39in/1m S12in/30cm | Queen Anne's lace; small white flowers | Su | 3–7 | ✳✳✳ | widespread |
| *Hemerocallis flava* | H/S3ft/90cm | Fragrant lemon-yellow flowers | Su | 3–10 | ✳✳✳ | China |
| *Iris sibirica* | H20–48in/0.5–1.2m S8in/20cm | Likes damp grass; blue-purple flowers | Su | 4–9 | ✳✳ | C.E. Europe |
| *Leucanthemum vulgare* | H12–36in/30–90cm S24in/60cm | Oxeye daisy; white and yellow daisies | LSu/ | 3–8 | ✳✳✳ | Europe/Asia |
| *Solidago sphacelata* | H/S18–24in/45–60cm | Goldenrod; arching panicles of yellow flowers | Au | 5–9 | ✳✳ | N. America |

### PRAIRIE MEADOWS

| | | | | | | |
|---|---|---|---|---|---|---|
| *Aster novae-angliae* | H3–5ft/1–1.5m S2ft/60cm | New England aster; yellow-centered daisies | LSu/LA | 4–9 | ✳✳ | N. America |
| *Boltonia asteroides* | H3–6ft/1–2m S3ft/1m | Masses of white yellow-centered flowers | LSu/A | 4–9 | ✳✳ | C. & E. USA |
| *Echinacea purpurea* | H60in/1.5m S18in/45cm | Purple coneflower; purple, partly reflexed daisy flowers | Su | 3–9 | ✳✳✳ | Eurasia |

| BOTANICAL NAME | HEIGHT AND SPREAD | DESCRIPTION | SEASON | ZONES | HARDINESS | ORIGIN |
|---|---|---|---|---|---|---|
| *Echinops ritro* | H24in/60cm S18in/45cm | Globe thistle; compact silvery plant | LSu | 3–9 | ✳✳✳ | C.E. Europe |
| *Eupatorium purpureum* | H0.75in/2cm S39in/1m | Joe Pye weed; tall pink-purple flowers; purple-tinged green leaves | LSu/A | 3–9 | ✳✳✳ | E. USA |
| *Helenium autumnale* | H3–5ft/1–1.5m S2ft/60cm | Sneezeweed; masses of daisylike flowers | LSu/A | 4–8 | ✳✳ | Canada, E. USA |
| *Liatris spicata* | H3–5ft/1–1.5m S2ft/60cm | Spike gayfeather; erect, wandlike spikes of purple-pink or white flowers | LSu/A | 4–9 | ✳✳ | E. & S. USA |
| *Panicum virgatum* | H/S3ft/1m S2–3ft/60–90cm | Switchgrass; upright clumps of leaves; good yellow fall color; purplish seed heads | All | 5–9 | ✳✳ | S. Canada, C. USA |
| *Ratibida pinnata* | H4ft/1.2m S18in/45cm | Grayhead coneflower; yellow daisy flowers with raised brown disks | Su/A | 3–10 | ✳✳✳ | N. America, Mexico |
| *Rudbeckia fulgida* | H36in/90cm S18in/45cm | Bright orange-yellow daisies; 'Herbstsonne' recommended | Su/A | 4–9 | ✳✳ | S.E. USA |
| *Thalictrum aquilegifolium* | H39in/1m S18in/45cm | Meadow rue; fluffy pink flowers; delicate fernlike leaves | Su | 5–9 | ✳✳ | Europe to Asia |
| *Verbascum chaixii 'Album'* | H36in/90cm S18in/45cm | Woolly-stemmed plant with dense white flowers | Su | 5–9 | ✳✳ | E.S. Europe |

## WOODLAND EDGE

### SHRUBS

| | | | | | | |
|---|---|---|---|---|---|---|
| *Aesculus parviflora* | H10ft/3m S15ft/5m | Bottlebrush buckeye; erect, spidery white flower clusters; yellow fall color; suckers | Su | 5–9 | ✳✳ | S.E. USA |
| *Clethra alnifolia* | H/S8ft/2.5m | Sweet pepperbush; dense upright clusters of small, fragrant bell-shaped, white flowers; oval leaves are toothed spreads by suckers | LSu/A | 3–9 | ✳✳✳ | E. USA |
| *Kalmia latifolia* | H/S10ft/3m | Mountain laurel; evergreen; clusters of white, pink, or pink-and-white flowers | LSp/ Su | 5–9 | ✳✳ | E. USA |
| *Viburnum lantana* | H/S10ft/3m | Wayfaring tree; deciduous shrub with white flowers; red berries | Su | 4–8 | ✳✳ | Europe, N. America, Asia |

### PERENNIALS

| | | | | | | |
|---|---|---|---|---|---|---|
| *Aquilegia vulgaris* | H36in/90cm S18in/45cm | Columbine; originals blue—many shaded culltivars | Su | 3–8 | ✳✳✳ | Europe |
| *Astrantia major* | H26in/70cm S18in/45cm | Silver-pink starry flowers | Su | 4–7 | ✳✳ | Eurasia |
| *Digitalis purpurea* | H6.5ft/2m S18in/45cm | Foxglove; pink or white bells | LSu | 4–9 | ✳✳ | Europe |
| *Dryopteris filix-mas* | H/S3ft/1m | Male fern; handsome clumps of mid-green fronds | Su/A | 4–8 | ✳✳ | Europe, N. America |

*Asplenium trichomanes*

*Vicia cracia*

*Thalictrum aquilegifolium*

| BOTANICAL NAME | HEIGHT AND SPREAD | DESCRIPTION | SEASON | ZONES | HARDINESS | ORIGIN |
|---|---|---|---|---|---|---|
| *Geranium phaeum* | H32in/80cm S18in/45cm | Dusky cranesbill; purple-maroon flowers | Su | 4–8 | ** | Europe |
| *Gillenia trifoliata* | H39in/1m S24in/60cm | Bowman's root; red stems; white flowers | Su | 5–9 | ** | N. America |
| *Lysimachia punctata* | H39in/1m S12in/30cm | Yellow loosestrife; whorls of yellow flowers | Su | 4–8 | ** | Europe |
| *Phlox divaricata* | H12–14in/30–35cm S20in/50cm | Wild blue phlox; semievergreen; fragrant, lilac or white flowers; self-sows | LSp/Su | 4–8 | ** | Canada, E. USA |
| *Tiarella cordifolia* | H8in/20cm S12in/30cm | Foamflower; profuse white flowers; bright green leaves | Su | 3–7 | *** | N. America |

### BULBS AND TUBERS

| | | | | | | |
|---|---|---|---|---|---|---|
| *Erythronium* species | H4–12in/10–30cm S4in/10cm | Dogtooth violet, trout lily; glossy-leaved plants with pink lilylike flowers with thrown-back sepals | Sp | 3–9 | *** | Europe, N. California |
| *Galanthus nivalis* | H8in/20cm S3in/8cm | Snowdrop; white drop flowers | ESp | 3–9 | *** | Europe |
| *Hyacinthoides non-scripta* | H12in/30cm S3in/8cm | English bluebell; pendent, bell-shaped flowers; naturalizes well | Sp | 4–9 | ** | Europe |
| *Narcissus pseudonarcissus* | H12in/30cm S6in/15cm | Wild daffodil; *N. cyclamineus* also naturalizes well | Sp | 3–8 | *** | Europe |

## DRY SHADE

### SHRUBS AND PERENNIALS

| | | | | | | |
|---|---|---|---|---|---|---|
| *Epimedium* species | H6–24in/15–60cm | Barrenwort; evergreen/semievergreen | ESp/LA | 5–9 | ** | E. Asia |
| *Geranium macrorrhizum* | H18in/45cm S24in/60cm | Bigroot geranium; pink flowers; scented leaves | ESu | 4–8 | ** | S. Europe |
| *Hosta* species and cultivars | H2–36in/5–90cm S1–5ft/30–150cm | Lavender or white flowers; handsome, often variegated foliage | Su/A | 3–8 | *** | Asia |
| *Iris foetidissima* | H/S24in/60cm | Long, narrow evergreen leaves; orange seed pods | Su | 7–9 | * | Europe, Africa |
| *Lunaria annua* | H36in/90cm S12in/30cm | Honesty; purple-flowered annual or biennial; decorative seed pods | Sp/Su | 5–9 | ** | Europe |
| *Rubus* 'Betty Ashburner' | H12in/30cm S spreading | Evergreen; prostrate, dark glossy leaves | Su | 7–9 | * | hybrid |
| *Symphytum ibericum* | H12in/30cm S spreading | Ovate, midgreen leaves; cream red-tipped flowers | LSp | 5–9 | ** | Caucasus |
| *Trachystemon orientalis* | H24in/60cm S18in/45cm | Large leaves; blue-purple flowers | Su | 7–10 | * | E. Europe |
| *Vinca minor* | H8in/20cm S spreading | Dwarf periwinkle; evergreen, sprawling foliage; blue or white flowers | Sp/Su | 2–9 | *** | Europe, Russia |

*Astrantia major*

*Erythronium revolutum*

*Crocosmia masoniorum*

| BOTANICAL NAME | HEIGHT AND SPREAD | DESCRIPTION | SEASON | ZONES | HARDINESS | ORIGIN |
|---|---|---|---|---|---|---|

## WATER AND WETLAND

### AQUATIC

| BOTANICAL NAME | HEIGHT AND SPREAD | DESCRIPTION | SEASON | ZONES | HARDINESS | ORIGIN |
|---|---|---|---|---|---|---|
| *Azolla filiculoides* | H0.5in/1cm S spreading mat | Fairy moss; lacy green, red in the fall | All | 7–11 | ✳ | N.S. America |
| *Iris laevigata* 'Variegata' | H30in/75cm S12in/30cm | Ivory variegation; blue flowers | Su | 4–9 | ✳✳ | E. Asia |
| *Iris pseudacorus* | H3ft/90cm S18in/45cm | Yellow flag; yellow with brown marks | Sp/Su | 5–8 | ✳✳ | Europe |
| *Lemna* species | H0.5in/1cm S spreading mat | Duckweed; tiny green floating plants that make a green mat | All | 4–9 | ✳✳ | cosmopolitan |
| *Menyanthes trifoliata* | H12in/30cm S spreading | Bogbean; fluffy pink flowers; trifoliate leaves | Su | 3–7 | ✳✳✳ | Europe, Asia, N. America |
| *Nymphaea* species | H6in/15cm S spreading | Water lilies; different cultivars for deep or shallow water | Su | 4–11 | ✳✳ | Eurasia, N. Africa |
| *Nymphoides peltata* | H6in/15cm S spreading | Fringed water lily; yellow flowers; very rapid spreader | Su | 5–11 | ✳✳ | Europe, Asia nat. USA |

### BOGS AND DAMP SOIL

| BOTANICAL NAME | HEIGHT AND SPREAD | DESCRIPTION | SEASON | ZONES | HARDINESS | ORIGIN |
|---|---|---|---|---|---|---|
| *Astilbe* hybrids | H18–36in/45–90cm S28in/70cm | Astilbe; tall frothy flowers in pinks and creams | Su | 4–8 | ✳✳ | E. Asia, N. America |
| *Caltha palustris* | H12in/30cm 18in/45cm | Marsh marigold; gold cups; glossy leaves; self-sows | Sp | 3–7 | ✳✳✳ | Europe, N. America |
| *Crocosmia masoniorum* | H39in/1m grown in clumps | Fanned leaves; arched red flower spikes; requires well-drained soil | Su | 5–9 | ✳✳ | S. Africa |
| *Darmera peltata* | H/S4ft/1.2m | Clusters of small pink flowers; large rounded leaves, 24in/60cm across; spreads slowly by rhizomes | LSp/ Su | 5–9 | ✳✳ | N.W. USA |
| *Filipendula rubra* | H8ft/2.5m S4ft/1.2m | Queen of the prairies; tall perennial with rose-pink flowers | Su | 3–9 | ✳✳✳ | E. America |
| *Filipendula ulmaria* | H5ft/1.5m S2ft/60cm | Meadowsweet; creamy, frothy flowers on stem tops | Su | 3–9 | ✳✳✳ | Europe, W. Asia |
| *Lysimachia nummularia* | H2in/5cm S spreading | Creeping Jenny; trailing stems small yellow flowers | Su | 4–8 | ✳✳ | Europe, nat. E. America |
| *Lychnis flos-cuculi* | H/S30in/75cm | Ragged robin; deep pink flowers | Su | 6–9 | ✳ | Europe, Siberia |
| *Lysichiton americanus* | H39in/1m S4ft/1.2m | Skunk cabbage; large leaves, saillike, yellow spathes; vigorous | Sp | 7–9 | ✳ | N.W. America |

### TREES FOR DAMP SOIL

| BOTANICAL NAME | HEIGHT AND SPREAD | DESCRIPTION | SEASON | ZONES | HARDINESS | ORIGIN |
|---|---|---|---|---|---|---|
| *Alnus glutinosa* | H80ft/25m S30ft/10m | Common alder; grows well in wet conditions such as pond sides | All | 3–7 | ✳✳✳ | Europe to Siberia |
| *Populus balamifera* | H to100ft/30m S15ft/5m | Balsam poplar; bright green balsam-scented, young leaves | Sp/ Su | 5–9 | ✳✳ | N. America |
| *Salix* 'Erythroflexuosa' | H15ft/5m S10ft/3m | Twisted willow; twisted shoots; bright green curly leaves | All | 5–9 | ✳✳ | Asia, China |
| *Taxodium distichum* | H70–130ft/20–40m S20–28ft/6–9m | Bald cypress; deciduous conifer; dainty foliage | All | 5–10 | ✳✳ | S.E. America |

### SHRUBS FOR DAMP SOIL

| BOTANICAL NAME | HEIGHT AND SPREAD | DESCRIPTION | SEASON | ZONES | HARDINESS | ORIGIN |
|---|---|---|---|---|---|---|
| *Hydrangea arborescens* | H/S8ft/2.5m | Creamy flowers held in large groups; broad oval leaves | LSu | 4–9 | ✳✳ | E. America |
| *Physocarpus opulifolius* | H/S4ft/1.2m spreading | 'Dart's Gold' ninebark; deciduous, small white flowers; prefers acidic soil | ESu | 3–7 | ✳✳✳ | N. America |
| *Sambucus nigra* f. *laciniata* | H/S8ft/2.5m | Cut-leaved elder; dark green finely cut leaves; white flowers in flat heads | ESu | 6–8 | ✳ | Europe, S.W. Asia |

# Index

# Acknowledgments

The Publisher would like to thank the following for their kind permission to reproduce the photographs in this book:

Key : **t** top, **c** centre, **b** bottom, **l** left, **r** right

Endpapers Garden Picture Library/Ron Evans; 1 S & O Mathews; 2 Andrew Lawson Photography/Anne Dexter; 3 Andrew Lawson Photography; 4-5 Garden Picture Library/J S Sira; 6-7 S & O Mathews; 8 Garden Picture Library/Ron Sutherland; 9 Garden Picture Library/J S Sira; 10 Andrew Lawson Photography/Eastgrove Cottage; 11 Bruce Coleman Ltd/Andy Purcell; 12 Andrew Lawson Photography; 13 **t** Francesca Greenoak; **b** Clive Nichols Photography/designer: Julie Toll; 14 Garden Picture Library/Lamontagne; 15 Garden Picture Library/Kathy Charlton; 16 Garden Picture Library/Henk Dijkman; 17 **t** Andrew Lawson Photography; **b** Andrew Lawson Photography; 18 **l** S & O Mathews, **r** Andrew Lawson Photography; 19 Jerry Harpur; 20 **t** Garden Picture Library/Alan Bedding; **b** Andrew Lawson Photography/Designer Anne Dexter; 22 Garden Picture Library/Jerry Pavia; 23 Andrew Lawson Photography; 24 Clive Nichols Photography/Designer:Mark Brown; 25 **t** Francesca Greenoak; **b** Garden Picture Library/Lamontagne; 26 S & O Mathews; 27 S & O Mathews; 28 **t** Andrew Lawson Photography; **b** S & O Mathews; 29 Jerry Harpur/Dolwen; 30 **l** Bruce Coleman Ltd/Sir Jeremy Grayson; **r** Francesca Greenoak; 31 Garden Picture Library/Steven Wooster; 32 Francesca Greenoak; 33 Reed Consumer Books Limited/Stephen Robson; 34 Garden Picture Library/John Glover; 35 Garden Picture Library/Sunniva Harte; 36 Jerry Harpur/Mr and Mrs Boyle, Home Farm, Blascote; 37 Garden Picture Library/Clive Boursnell; 38 Garden Picture Library/Marijke Heuff; 39 **l** Garden Picture Library/Michael Howes; **r** Jerry Pavia; 40 Jerry Pavia; 41 Andrew Lawson Photography; 42-43 S & O Mathews; 44 Andrew Lawson Photography; 45 Andrew Lawson Photography; 46 **t** Francesca Greenoak; **b** Andrew Lawson Photography; 48 S & O Mathews; 49 S & O Mathews; 50 Andrew Lawson Photography; 51 S & O Mathews; 52 Clive Nichols Photography/Greystone Cottage, Oxon; 53 Clive Nichols Photography; 54 Garden Picture Library/Sunniva Harte; 55 Garden Picture Library/Ron Evans; 56 Clive Nichols Photography/Abbotswood, Gloucestershire; **r** Andrew Lawson Photography; 57 S & O Mathews; 58 Garden Picture Library/Ron Sutherland; 59 S & O Mathews; 61 Garden Picture Library/Steven Wooster; 63 S & O Mathews; 64 S & O Mathews; 65 **t** Garden Picture Library/Ron Sutherland; **b** Clive Nichols Photography/Painswick Rococo Garden, Glos.; 66 Andrew Lawson Photography/Denmans Gardens; 67 Jerry Harpur/designer: Molly Love, CA; 68 S & O Mathews; 70 **l** Andrew Lawson Photography; **r** Andrew Lawson Photography; 71 S & O Mathews; 72 **t** S & O Mathews; **b** S & O Mathews; 73 Garden Picture Library/Juliette Wade; 74 S & O Mathews; 75 **t** Jerry Harpur/designer: D Gaboulaud; **b** Andrew Lawson Photography; 76 Garden Picture Library/Jerry Pavia; 77 **t** Garden Picture Library/John Glover; **b** S & O Mathews; 78 Garden Picture Library/Lamontagne; 79 **l** Jerry Harpur/designer: Roger Raiche, S.F.; **r** Andrew Lawson Photography; 80 Jerry Harpur/Great Dixter; 81 Andrew Lawson Photography; 83 Garden Picture Library/Kathy Charlton; 84 Jerry Harpur/Great Dixter; 85 **t** S & O Mathews; **b** Francesca Greenoak; 86 S & O Mathews; 87 **t** Andrew Lawson Photography/The Garden House/Buclkand Monachorum, Devon; **b** S & O Mathews; 88 **t** Garden Picture Library/Ron Evans; **b** Andrew Lawson Photography; 89 Jerry Harpur/designer: Mirabel Osler; 90 Applewood Seed Company.; 91 Applewood Seed Company.; 92 Garden Picture Library/Gary Rogers; 93 **t** Bruce Coleman Ltd/John Shaw; **b** Garden Picture Library/J S Sira; 94-5 Clive Nichols Photography/designer: H M P Leyhill; 96 Andrew Lawson Photography; 97 Garden Picture Library/JS Sira; 98 Garden Picture Library/John Glover; 99 Jerry Harpur; 100 **l** S & O Mathews; **r** Andrew Lawson Photography/designer: Arne Maynard;101 S & O Mathews; 102 Garden Picture Library/Sunniva Harte; 103 **t** Garden Picture Library/John Miller; **b** Reed Consumer Books Limited/Stephen Robson/Occidental Arts and Ecology Centre, California; 104 Garden Picture Library/Henk Dijkman; 105 **t** Garden Picture Library/Artist: Peter Gough Ph:Sunniva Harte; **b** William Pye; 106 Jerry Harpur; 107 Andrew Lawson Photography; 108 **t** Andrew Lawson Photography; **b** Stiffkey Lamp Shop; 110 S & O Mathews; 111 Garden Picture Library/Mayer/Le Scanff; 112 Garden Picture Library/Juliet Greene; 113 Garden Picture Library/Mayer/Le Scanff; 114 **t** Francesca Greenoak; **b** Garden Picture Library/Brigitte Thomas; 115 Garden Picture Library/JS Sira; 116 N.H.P.A./Stephen Dalton; 117 Andrew Lawson Photography; 118 S & O Mathews; 119 **t** Reed Consumer Books Limited/Stephen Robson; **b** N.H.P.A./Robert Erwin; 121 Andrew Lawson Photography; 122 Jerry Harpur/desgner: Mirabel Osler; 123 Andrew Lawson Photography; 124 **l** N.H.P.A./Laurie Campbell; **r** Bruce Coleman Ltd/G. Ziesler; 125 **t** Bruce Coleman Ltd/Mike Price; **b** Aquila Photographics/Wayne Lankinen; 126 Aquila Photographics/Abraham Cardwell; 127 S & O Mathews; 128 S & O Mathews; 129 Aquila Photographics/A.H.Vanhinsbergh; 130 Garden Picture Library/Brigitte Thomas; 131 Andrew Lawson Photography; 132 **l** Jerry Harpur/Designer: Susan Horseman; **r** S & O Mathews; 134 Garden Picture Library/John Glover; 135 Andrew Lawson Photography; 136 Garden Picture Library/Michael Howes; 137 **t** Garden Picture Library/Juliette Wade, **b** Andrew Lawson Photography/The Mythic Garden; 138 S & O Mathews; 139 Garden Picture Library/J S Sira; 140 Andrew Lawson Photography; 141 Jerry Harpur; 142 Garden Picture Library/Jerry Pavia; 143 **l** Garden Picture Library/J S Sira; **r** Garden Picture Library/Brian Carter; 144 **b** S & O Mathews; 145 Andrew Lawson Photography; 146 Garden Picture Library/Marijke Heuff; 147 Garden Picture Library/Geoff Dann; 148-9 Jerry Harpur 150 **l** Garden Picture LIbrary/Sunniva Harte; **c** Garden Picture Library/Vaughan Fleming; **r** Andrew Lawson Photography; 153 **l** Garden Picture Library/Howard Rice; **c** Francesca Greenoak; **r** Garden Picture Library/Ron Evans; 154 **l** Andrew Lawson Photography; **c** Garden Picture Library/JS Sira; **r** Andrew Lawson Photography.